# Puppy Parenting

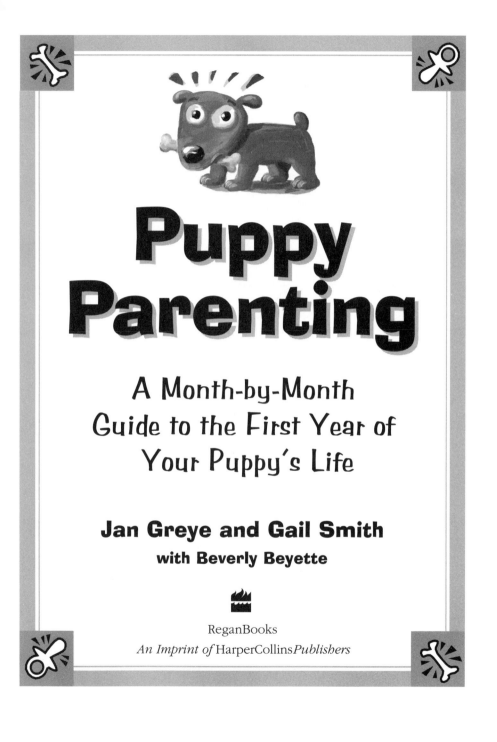

# Puppy Parenting

## A Month-by-Month Guide to the First Year of Your Puppy's Life

### Jan Greye and Gail Smith

#### with Beverly Beyette

ReganBooks
*An Imprint of* HarperCollins*Publishers*

HarperCollins books may be purchased for educational, business,
or sales promotional use.
For information please write: Special Markets Department,
HarperCollins Publishers Inc., 10 East 53rd Street, New York, NY 10022.

FIRST EDITION

*Designed by Kate Nichols*
*Illustrations by Will Weston*

Printed on acid-free paper

Library of Congress Cataloging-in-Publication Data

Greye, Jan.
Puppy parenting : a month-by-month guide to the first year of your
puppy's life / Jan Greye and Gail Jesse Smith.
p.    cm.
Includes bibliographical references (p.   ).
ISBN 0-06-039315-7
1. Puppies. 2. Puppies—Development. I. Smith, Gail Jesse. II. Title.
SF427 .G764 2001
636.7'07—dc21        2001019191

01  02  03  04  05  RRD  10  9  8  7  6  5  4  3  2  1

**O**f all the dogs that have owned us,
or have allowed us to take care of them, three have
a special place in our hearts.

**T**his book is dedicated to

### Slither,

our Border Collie mix,
for her patience and devotion;

### Mr. Murphy,

our Toy Poodle,
for his undying love and understanding; and

### Marble,

a Hound mix,
who brought us joy just by letting us
share her life.

**W**e thank them, and we promise always to listen to
the heartbeat at our feet.

**W**e also dedicate this book to
the following wonderful dogs, some of the "furry children"
the Kritter Sitters have been privileged to
have entrusted to our care:

Argyle, Ashley, August, Bailey, Bentley, Bernice,
Bizet, Bleu, Bob, Bogie, Bogey and Bacall, Buckwheat, Buster, Carla, Cassie,
Chelsea, Chrissy, C.J., Clancy, Clayre, Cleo, Daisy, Daisy June, Dakota,
Dustin, Dusty, Fayga, Gabby, Gizmo, Goldie, Gracie, Gremmie, Harley, Harlow,
Hildy, Jake, Jerry, Joey, Kali, Lady, Leo, Lexi, Lilly, Linda, Lola,
Lucy, Luke, Mac, Maddy, Madison, Maggie, Marble, the three Maxes, Mia,
Minute, Misty, Molly, Morgan, Murphy, Nicholas, Nikki, Olive,
Oliver, Otis, Peepers, Pepper, Puka, Rags, Sadie, Sammi, Sammy,
Sedona, Toadi, Thurston, Toni, Winston, and Woosie.

# Contents

**Index**   193

# Acknowledgments

**T**he Kritter Sitters would like to thank Judith Regan for convincing us to write this book and Renée Iwaszkiewicz, our editor at ReganBooks, for patiently and skillfully shepherding *Puppy Parenting* to completion.

We are grateful to Dee Chester, Lyn King, Leigh Layne, and Steven and Karen Pollock for their input, support, and encouragement.

Thanks, too, to these caring dog owners, our clients: Ryan and Elizabeth Botev, Jill Carter, Don and Britt Chadwick, David and Megan Dills, Iris Dugow, Kim Ellesser, Rosanne Garcia, Jim and Diane Goldberg, Thelma Harris, Shelly Kamanitz, Curtis and Gabrielle Kemeny, Peter and Kate Klausner, Doug and Nora MacLellan, Donna Manders, Jerry and Valerie Pearlman, Dan and Lisa Platt, Mikki Polan, Alan and Carol Mendel, John and Vicki Rosenberg, Hugo Rossitter, Cindy Sarnoff, Sydney Silverman, Erwin and Carin Sokol, Ted Stafford, Richard and Debra Stambul,

Robert and Linda Weinstein, Hutton and Ruth Wilkinson, and Bob and Barbara Wold.

Dr. M. J. Brandt and Dr. Sandy Milo at Bay Cities Veterinary Hospital in Marina del Rey, California; Dr. Stephen J. Fynaardt at VCA Clamar Animal Hospital in Torrance, California; and Dr. William F. Carlsen at Carlsen Animal Hospital in West Los Angeles have been there for us and our dogs in emergencies large and small, always ready to share their professional expertise.

# Puppy Parenting

# Introduction

# The Best Bed 'N Bone Joint in Town

**P**eople call us the Beverly Hills Dog Divas, a name given us by a client because so many of our four-footed charges live in the fabled 90210 zip code. More formally, we're proprietors of Kritter Sitters—babysitters, companions, and confidantes to a Noah's Ark of pets that at any given time is apt to include a dozen doggie houseguests in our home. Big dogs, little dogs, fancy dogs, pound dogs.

Now, no one has a sudden epiphany, waking up one morning and deciding, "When I grow up, I'm going to run a bed-and-breakfast for dogs!" But we saw a need. So many people were reluctant to kennel their animals and, as animal lovers and dog owners, we understood why they wanted the best, and most loving, environment for their dogs when they had to be away from home. Maybe we're both locked into the Peter Pan syndrome and are never going to grow up.

We also take care of cats (in their own homes, for reasons obvious to any cat person). And we've babysat a pygmy goat, clipped the nails of a client's fourteen cockatiels, sung "Happy Birthday" to a parrot until he finally stopped squawking "Sing It Again, Sam," and been foster parents to an oversexed turtle named Yertl.

One day a woman called and said, "I have two otters. . . ." All we could say was, "Why?" How do you cuddle up to an otter? But there they were, living in her bathtub, and there we were, coming every day to feed them.

We've provided TLC for a raccoon named Rocky and for a really ugly iguana, but we turned down a tarantula—we're not really into spiders—and we don't do snakes. We're just not going to find ourselves feeding Miss Minnie Mouse to somebody's boa constrictor.

Most of what we know about dogs we've learned from dogs. Take George, the Bernese Mountain Dog, for example. Now, his owner had assured us that George wouldn't dream of slipping out of the house when we came to feed him. So what did George do but whiz past us the minute we opened the door and lead us on a Keystone Kops chase through the streets of Santa Monica with onlookers shouting, "He went thataway!" We're definitely not jogger types and that dog could boogie. With one of us on foot, the other following in the car, and both of us screaming, "George, George, where are you!" we cut quite a swath through the beach city and might still be chasing George had he not decided that the game was over and trotted home, leaving us in his dust. The moral of this story: Take the time to really get to know your dog and his habits.

Some clients, such as George's owner, prefer to have their dogs tended in their own homes and they give us a set of keys. Once, a producer and longtime client had to leave town on a moment's notice. She'd left a new key for us in the backyard under one of those little gray rocks that are supposed to fool burglars. What she didn't tell us was that she'd just had her yard landscaped—with about two hundred little gray rocks. Two dogs and three cats stared at us in disbelief through the French doors, meowing and barking, as we sifted through piles of rocks.

Nothing surprises us today, but when we went into the pet care business in 1986 we weren't quite prepared for dogs that are more pampered than most people's children. New clients in Benedict Canyon, a rather tony area on the Westside of Los Angeles, took us literally when we suggested that their pair of Golden Retrievers needed their own space. They promptly had a spacious cottage built for them—with air-conditioning. Now, we are not telling you that you need to have a doggie condo for your precious pooch. Puppy parenting is not about buying the best of everything. It's about providing the best care and giving lots of love.

Vacationing clients call from London, Rome, and Tokyo, from ships and from private planes, just to make sure their dogs are well and happy. We've had to break some callers of wanting to talk to their beloveds, explaining that it's a little like calling a kid at camp—a dog doesn't want to come home until it hears Mom's or Dad's voice. Nevertheless, some clients have insisted that we hand over the telephone so they could sing "Happy Birthday" to Buster, Bailey, Bogey, or Bacall.

Skeptics can't believe that a dozen dogs, some of them strange to one another, have coexisted happily and peacefully in our house together with our resident pillow princesses, Mona the cat, Ashley the Maltese, and Mr. Murphy, an aging Poodle with an attitude bigger than the Grand Canyon. But they have, and that's because we screen potential clients to winnow out the troublemakers, dogs that have not been properly socialized, and aggressive dogs, including unneutered males. We've had failures. We had to tell one client at the last minute, "Sorry, you can't go to Hawaii. Please come and get your dog." That dog was a terror. We've had biters, cat haters, dogs so hyper they appeared to be on crack, fiercely territorial dogs, spoiled dogs, and destructive dogs, all of whose owners had smiled brightly and assured us, "Oh, he gets along just fine with other animals. . . ."

There are wired dogs and laid-back dogs, shy dogs and outgoing dogs. We're not really into doggie astrology, but there are those who will tell you that there is a cosmically correct pooch for everyone (Schnauzers for Sagittarians, French Poodles for Libras—well, you get the idea). We think there are better ways to help you choose the breed that suits your personality and lifestyle.

In these pages we share with you what we've learned over the past fifteen years from our "perfect" dogs and "problem" dogs. You will learn to teach your puppy with a smile. But for the most part, guests at the Best Bed 'N Bone Joint in Town (a name coined by a grateful client) live happily ever after—or at least for the two weeks until Mom and Dad get home from vacation.

That's because they are dogs that have been properly chosen, trained, and socialized. In this book we will tell you how to raise a socially acceptable, loving dog that will reward you with years of faithful companionship. There's nothing more fun than bringing up a puppy— if you do it right.

We wrote this book because we wanted you, the first-time dog owner, not to take raising a puppy so seriously that all the fun goes out of it. Puppy parenting is not a science. Just follow your heart—and use a little common sense—and you and your puppy will do fine. There are some do's and don'ts, of course, and we have explained those to you.

Above all, we don't want you to lose sight of the fact that having a puppy is fun. Don't be intimidated just because you've read some dog book that tried to convince you that a puppy needs a $1,000 layette and a Santa's bag full of toys.

What a puppy needs is a loving home and someone to teach him the manners that will make him your devoted companion, eager to please and a pleasure to have around. And—who knows—you may live a longer, healthier life if you have a dog. A University of Buffalo study of forty-eight stockbrokers, all of whom lived alone and had high blood pressure, showed that they responded much better to stress and had significantly lower blood pressure only six months after letting a dog or cat into their lives. Another study showed that heart attack survivors live longer if they have pets.

We have babysat hundreds of dogs, including a few ill-mannered little devils. We know that a happy dog-owner relationship starts with the right dog match. You will learn to teach your puppy with a smile on your face (even if the pup's just piddled on your priceless Oriental), to guide him with understanding, compassion, and patience, patience, patience. You and your puppy are entering into a partnership—he needs to be controlled, not broken. Good luck and five pads up!

Jan and Jesse

# Should You Have a Dog?

How much is that doggie in the window? Don't even ask. Puppies are not impulse purchases. Puppies should never be bought because they're "so cute." That irresistible little bundle of fluff with the limpid brown eyes may grow up to be 200 pounds of dog galumphing through your house.

Before we help you choose the right breed for you, and the right breeder, we want you to know that having a dog is a big responsibility, as well as a great joy. Dogs are loving, loyal, and intelligent. Dogs still love you if you pack on a few too many pounds or lose a lucrative account. But, in return, you must be willing to give of your time and to give up life as you knew it pre-puppy to give this little ball of fur your love and support. A puppy doesn't stop needing attention just because you're tired or busy. Come rain or shine, he needs to be exercised. Away from his mother and littermates, he will look to you to provide love, affection, and discipline. You are the one who must teach him right from wrong. If you want a perfectly behaved dog, we suggest a stuffed one. If you don't have the patience to teach your dog manners, maybe you should think about getting a cat or tropical fish. Some people just aren't meant to be dog owners.

## Are You Really Ready for a Puppy?

Here's a little checklist to help you decide whether to bring a puppy into your life. Be honest in answering the questions. A dog is not a status symbol. A dog is a commitment.

- ✔ How many adults are there in your family? Where there are two adults, the puppy will be less apt to be left alone for long periods.
- ✔ Are there children under the age of five in the household? Very

young children do not understand how to interact with puppies (think ear pulling) and may cause the puppy to become
either nippy or timid.

✔ Is your daily work schedule eight hours or fewer? More than
eight hours? Puppies need to spend a lot of time with their new
owners.

✔ Do you spend your leisure time being physically active—jogging, walking, etc.? Or do you prefer to read, do needlepoint,
or play Bingo?

✔ Will you have read up on the breeds you are considering before buying a pup?

✔ Are you willing to spend the time and money to see that your
puppy gets his shots on schedule and has regular checkups
and tooth cleanings?

✔ Are there cats or other not-so-dog-friendly pets in the household? Fish don't count.

✔ Do you live in a house, a condominium, or an apartment? If
you plan to get a small dog, a condo or an apartment is not a
minus.

✔ If you want a high-maintenance breed, are you willing to invest the time and money to have your dog professionally
groomed on a regular basis?

✔ Are you willing to spend quality time with your new puppy,
making sure he will be included in the family circle? Dogs are
very sociable.

✔ Are you willing to have your dog spayed or neutered?

✔ If you decide on a guard or protection dog, such as a
Rottweiler, Doberman Pinscher, or German Shepherd, are you
committed to having the dog professionally trained?

✔ Do you have the patience to crate-train your puppy? Crate
training, which we will explain to you later, is by far the best
method of housebreaking, but it does require patience and
repetition.

Once you've considered all these factors, you should have a pretty good idea whether you're ready to get a puppy. If you aren't, perhaps you can make adjustments in your life to make room for a dog. If you're not willing to be flexible, you might be better off getting a goldfish or taking up gardening.

# Narrowing the Search

As a prospective dog owner, you may find you don't fit neatly into any one category. Maybe you live in a tiny Manhattan apartment, but want a dog large and sturdy enough to jog with in Central Park. Here's another checklist to help you think about whether you really want a dog and, if you are sure you do, to help further narrow your search for the right dog for you:

- ✔ **You're just looking for a cuddly companion.** Go for one of the Toy breeds, such as a Maltese, Shih Tzu, Dachshund, Yorkshire Terrier, or Lhasa Apso.
- ✔ **You're looking for a watchdog.** A Rottweiler, German Shepherd, Great Dane, Doberman Pinscher, or Border Collie fits the bill.
- ✔ **You just want a loving, loyal dog that will be a true member of the family.** Good choices: the Golden Retriever, Labrador Retriever, Basset Hound, Bernese Mountain Dog, or Norwich Terrier.
- ✔ **You want a puppy that will be accepting of children.** The Bulldog, Labrador Retriever, Golden Retriever, and Bernese Mountain Dog are tot-tolerant. If the kids are older, consider a Rhodesian Ridgeback, Saint Bernard, Bichon Frise, Poodle, or Shetland Sheepdog. Definitely in the "no kids, please" category: American Eskimo Dog, German Wirehaired Pointer, Italian Greyhound, Borzoi, and Dandie Dinmont Terrier.

✔ **You want a puppy that thrives on lots of attention.** The Cavalier King Charles Spaniel, Keeshond, and English Foxhound lap it up. To a lesser degree, so do the Petit Basset Griffon Vendeen, Field Spaniel, and Manchester Terrier. The Affenpinscher, Jack Russell Terrier, and Airedale Terrier can take it or leave it.

✔ **You want a puppy that is very active.** Breeds guaranteed to wear you out in short order include the Australian Shepherd, Border Collie, Shetland Sheepdog, and Old English Sheepdog. Those that enjoy little more than an occasional walk include the Papillon, English Bulldog, Maltese, and Silky Terrier. The couch potatoes? The Chihuahua, Italian Greyhound, and Yorkshire Terrier.

✔ **You want a puppy that is independent.** Those that will do as you ask—if they happen to feel like it—include the Newfoundland, Irish Wolfhound, and Bedlington Terrier. By contrast, the Labrador Retriever, Golden Retriever, Bulldog, Border Collie, and Australian Shepherd are eager to please. The Rottweiler, Doberman Pinscher, and Bull Mastiff definitely have minds of their own.

✔ **You want a puppy that will bark on occasion, but will not drive you out of your mind with his yapping.** The Vizsla, Australian Terrier, and Labrador Retriever are pretty much strong, silent types. If you are truly bark-intolerant, go for a Basenji, a Bull Mastiff, or a Wheaten Terrier.

✔ **You want a puppy that needs professional grooming every three months or less.** Good choices: the Jack Russell Terrier, Saluki, Dachshund, Weimaraner, Welsh Terrier, and Boxer. The Bernese Mountain Dog, Swiss Mountain Dog, Labrador Retriever, Shetland Sheepdog, and Siberian Husky should make monthly forays to the beauty parlor. At the high end, typically requiring biweekly salon trips, are the Poodle, Maltese, Bichon Frise, Lhasa Apso, Pekingese, West Highland Terrier, and Cocker Spaniel.

Obviously, we've listed only some of the more popular breeds, but this should help steer you toward, or away from, certain breeds and other dogs in their groups.

## I'm a Little Fur Person

A puppy comes with a built-in set of demands: walk me, feed me, play with me, teach me. A puppy eats, poops and sleeps, eats, poops and sleeps. Owning a dog is like owning a little fur person. It's like having a baby in the house, except that you can diaper a baby.

Like a child, a dog is a long-term commitment. Depending upon breed and size, your pup will live on average from ten to fifteen years.

Dogs are different from cats. A cat may give you the time of day if she's in the mood, but a dog needs interaction with you, and needs it constantly. You are, in effect, his pack leader. A dog wants to be where you are, to watch every move you make.

## Hey! I'm No Trophy

A dog is not a trophy. A dog is both an emotional and a financial commitment. He is a member of the family. If you leave town, your dog must either be boarded or taken to a pet sitter. (That's us.) A dog must be bathed. A dog must be flea-proofed. A dog must be taken to the vet for his shots. A dog must have the proper licenses. Having a dog is not simply a matter of throwing a bone down on the floor and shutting the kitchen door.

All too often the adorable little puppy that comes into the family is banished to the backyard when he grows up and does things that are less than adorable. In most cases, the poor pooch is not at fault. His owners just weren't willing to commit the time to housebreak him and school him in basic obedience. There's nothing sadder than seeing a dog chained in a yard fourteen or even twenty-four hours a day, pacing back and forth on a tiny cement square. A dog sent into permanent exile in the yard may die of a broken heart. Or, out of sheer boredom and loneliness, he may start barking, chewing, and digging, assuring himself of a one-way ticket to the nearest animal shelter.

# I'm Not Ol' Yeller and I'm Not Rin-tin-tin: What Kind of Dog Is Right for You?

Right off, ignore that inner voice telling you that you must have a dog just like those perfect movie pooches. Remember: When Lassie came home, it wasn't to a two-bedroom condominium.

All too often, people choose a dog with their hearts. He's so cute, or he's got dots on his nose, or he reminds them of a dog they once had. Then they find out that they have bought themselves a dog that is going to eat them out of house and home, or whose haircuts cost more than theirs, or a dog of a breed given to some vile-sounding medical disorder.

When we do dog searches for our clients, frequently we have to steer them away from a breed that's totally unsuitable for them. One man, a type A personality and a workaholic, was dead-set on getting a Weimaraner. Now, the last thing this man needed was a Weimaraner, which is also an A personality. What he needed was a big, floppy "What, me worry?" dog. At our urging, he wound up with a Chocolate Lab, a dog to come home to and unwind with. It is a match made in heaven.

Often, people will have their hearts set on a certain breed, but before making a final decision will ask our advice. We always ask them why they want that breed. "Well, because they're so irresistible," they'll say. But it may be the wrong dog for them, and reality sets in when the cute phase is over and the dog is doing what comes naturally for his breed, maybe bolting out the door at every opportunity or nipping at the kids. They might have decided they couldn't live without a Shar-pei because of "all those adorable wrinkles." They had no idea how much work a Shar-pei is—or what Shar-peis do when they grow up. For one thing, they bite.

We winced when *101 Dalmatians* and its sequel came out, knowing that Dalmatians were going to be the flavor-of-the-month and that breeders would be turning out Dalmatians as though they were Beanie Babies. Now, Dalmatians are very nice dogs, but they're not for everyone. Dozens of these dogs wound up in shelters. When Jack Nicholson in *As Good As It Gets* had a love-hate relationship with a Brussels Griffon that was beyond cute, the dog world braced for a tsunami of Brussels Griffons.

## Nippers, Naughty Dogs, Nice Dogs

All puppies are darling. All puppies are not for you. Rottweilers, Akitas, and German Shepherds are A personalities. Cockers are nippers, nondiscriminating nippers that will bite anybody or anything that comes too close. It's not a killer kind of bite, just an "I want to be left alone" bite. "I want my space, so move on."

Border Collies and Australian Shepherds are both wonderful—but they are high-energy dogs that need to be kept busy or they'll be bouncing off the walls out of sheer boredom. And a bored dog is a dog that gets into trouble—chewing and digging. You may like to think of yourself as a jogger or biker, the type who should have a Frisbee-fetching dog, when in reality you like to come home, turn on the TV, and flop. What you need is a dog that just wants to lie there being stroked. Good candidates: Bulldogs, Lhasa Apsos (though they're a bit nippy), King

Charles Spaniels, Cocker Spaniels, Poodles, Malteses, and the somewhat yappy Silkies. Beagles definitely do not qualify.

As for the Jack Russell, a beguiling and currently very popular breed, your chance of wearing out a Jack Russell is about equal to that of your winning the lottery. These dogs have such A-plus personalities that they can't stand each other. Put two Jack Russells together and neither will back down. "I'm going to kick your butt." "No, I'm going to kick *your* butt." And they'll spend three weeks in a standoff. But let a Golden Retriever come on the scene and be accosted by the Jack Russell, and the Golden will just yawn and go, "Oh, hello, you freak." The Jack Russell will decide very quickly: "Oh, well, okay, fine. I can't intimidate you so I'll just have to be your buddy." Another word of caution about Jack Russells: Given any chance, they're out the door like a shot.

# Your Lifestyle: Athlete or Couch Potato?

The first thing to consider when choosing a breed is your lifestyle. Do you leap out of bed at dawn to jog on the beach, or is surfing the Internet your idea of strenuous exercise? Do you work at home or go to an office? Is home a house or an apartment? Are you out of town a great deal? Are you single or married? An A personality or a couch potato? How much time do you have to spend with a dog?

Whichever of these lifestyles defines you, there's a dog to match among our Top Ten breeds. We chose these dogs for their adaptability, ease of maintenance (no, a Poodle does not have to prance around with all those silly pom-poms), and because they are child-friendly. We point out the upsides and downsides of each breed. You may have your heart set on a Saint Bernard (which, by the way, is a notorious drooler) when common sense dictates that you get a Chihuahua.

Different breeds were bred originally for specific purposes. Although these dogs may no longer be used for those purposes, they retain many of the traits prized in their ancestors. And they may, or may not, be a match for your lifestyle. Hounds, bred as hunting dogs, tend to be hyper. The working breeds such as the Rottweiler were bred to pull carts and wagons and they need plenty of exercise. The Terriers originally were bred as ratters. They can't sit still for long—and they won't let you sit still, either.

Some of the best pets have no pedigrees. They are mutts. In the next chapter, we discuss the relative merits of bluebloods and "dog dogs."

## Kids and Canines

Are you getting a dog for a child? Although we have clients with dogs and babies cohabiting happily, we think a child should be at least five years old before the family gets a puppy. A dog will quickly size up a smaller child, decide that this little person is a littermate, not to be taken seriously, and will run roughshod over the child. Three- and four-year-olds are given to yanking a puppy's tail or riding a puppy as if he were a pony which, oddly enough, a puppy does tend to resent. And re-member—once the novelty wears off, you are the one who'll end up feeding the dog, walking the dog, and schlepping the dog around to all of his various appointments.

If there are young children in the household, don't pick a dog whose breed has a short lifespan. These children are going to be dev-astated at the loss of the family pet. If you're single and don't plan to marry, or to have children, fine—go for the Great Dane or another deep-chested dog with a life expectancy of no more than ten to twelve years. But if you have a child, a better choice is a Retriever or one of the smaller breeds, many of which live considerably longer. This will save the child a big heartache.

# Size Does Count

Do you want a big dog or a little dog? Maybe you want one and your spouse the other. There's room for negotiation. Most guys do like little dogs. They just don't want you to know that they do. We had this client, a hulking linebacker for the former Los Angeles Raiders, who had a Maltese that fit in the palm of his hand. That dog was the love of his life. We're partial to little dogs, especially Malteses and Poodles. The little dogs are so whimsical and funny, and have the most wonderful personalities.

You may prefer a large dog, but don't think you have space enough for one. A good choice might be a German Shepherd, which is not a runner, or even a Great Dane, which is really a house mouse. A client with a Great Dane chose to move from a house to a tiny apartment when her dog lost his sight. That big dog is doing much better within a confined space. As a rule, we don't recommend that someone occupying a studio apartment install a dog half the size of that apartment, but we had a German Shepherd boarder that was a good candidate. He wouldn't even chase a ball. He'd just kind of look at us like, "You go get it. If you think I'm going to run after that, you're crazy." Some of the Terriers actually need more space than the big breeds.

As a general rule, though, good-sized dogs and high-energy dogs do need a good-sized yard. Coop one of these dogs up all day in an apartment and he's going to be miserable—and probably naughty. A Toy breed is a great choice for apartment dwellers and for older people who really don't want to get out there and sprint in the park with their dog. But big-city folk dead-set on having a large dog can compensate by taking the dog to a park daily and letting him romp.

# Boy Dog or Girl Dog?

We admit to partiality to female dogs. Females, if spayed, are not roamers. They are calmer and less aggressive and, we've found, easier to train. On the other hand, a male dog makes a more assertive watchdog and, if neutered, an excellent pet. Males tend more to be one-person dogs, which is appealing to many men. Female dogs are more like little girls—they like to be hugged and cuddled—while male dogs are more like little boys and may resist all the huggy-kissy stuff—"Aw, c'mon, Mom. . . ."

# The Fur-Bearance Factor

There are high-maintenance dogs with a pricey grooming routine befitting a film goddess. Then there are what we call "wash-and-wear" dogs that do just fine with an occasional home shampoo and require no expensive clipping and trimming at Canine Coiffures.

Is it important to you to live in House Beautiful, or will you tolerate little clumps of fur on your burgundy velveteen settee? If you fancy yourself a Martha Stewart, this may be a good reason to consider one of the low-shedding breeds such as Dachshunds, which really don't have much fur. On the other hand, Jack Russells, though also short-haired, shed like crazy, as do Bulldogs. Malteses, although longhaired, aren't big shedders, but do require frequent bathing to keep those coats nice and white. The more you brush any dog, the less likely you'll be to have your clothes and sofa blanketed in fur. But if you like the breed, and the breed happens to be longhaired, you can always give your dog a short haircut. You're allowed—even if purists will be horrified.

Some dogs can be washed at home and towel-dried or blow-dried, and that's the end of it—no expensive weekly or biweekly trips to the groomer. These dogs include the Labs, Water Spaniels, Bluetick Hounds, and Bloodhounds. But all dogs should go to the groomer at least twice a year—and to one that hand-dries, not cage-dries, the dogs. How would you like to be locked in a small cage with a blow-dryer on a pedestal blasting hot air in your face?

# Tough to Train or Doggie Genius?

One of the questions we're asked most often is, "Which are the easiest dogs to train?" Some breeds are easier to train than others, but how a dog responds to schooling is largely a matter of physical build and temperament, not of native intelligence. We have cared for several hundred dogs and have found that all dogs will learn by trial and error. It doesn't take a canine quiz kid to repeat behaviors that bring good results—doggie treats, hugs, and kisses—and to avoid behaviors that result in scolding or punishment. Because these are dogs, not humans with fur, they do have limitations. A dog can't be trained to drive you to work after brewing your morning coffee, but he can learn to jump, sit, and fetch on command. Some are natural retrievers; some aren't. Don't expect to get a superdog that will do it all to perfection. And remember—harsh treatment will not make your dog "smarter." It will only make him fearful of you. Here is a partial listing of breeds and their "trainability."

These dogs are very easy to train:

- Australian Cattle Dog
- Border Collie
- Doberman Pinscher
- German Shepherd
- German Shorthaired Retriever
- Golden Retriever
- Labrador Retriever
- Poodle
- Rottweiler
- Schnauzer
- Siberian Husky
- Weimaraner

These dogs think training is a game and they tend to respond well:

- Airedale
- Australian Terrier
- Collie
- Jack Russell Terrier
- Old English Sheepdog
- Puli

These breeds are somewhat excitable and easily distracted. With proper motivation, they will train well:

- Bearded Collie
- Bedlington Terrier
- Belgian Shepherd
- Bichon Frise
- Brittany Spaniel
- Cairn Terrier
- Cavalier King Charles Spaniel
- Cocker Spaniel
- Fox Terrier
- Gordon Setter
- Keeshond
- Shetland Sheepdog
- West Highland Terrier

These are large dogs, and slower on their feet, but make up for lack of speed with reliability:

- Alaskan Malamute
- Bernese Mountain Dog
- Newfoundland
- Rhodesian Ridgeback

These dogs are very responsive for their size:

- Boxer
- Bull Terrier
- Staffordshire Bull Terrier

These breeds are hardheaded, and it takes patience to train them:

- Basenji
- Beagle
- Chow Chow
- Samoyed

These small dogs may appear flighty, but don't let appearances fool you. They can be trained very quickly:

- Chihuahua
- Corgis
- Maltese
- Papillon
- Pekingese
- Pomeranian

The physical conformation of these breeds limits their trainability. Just the basics are the best you can expect from them:

- Basset Hound
- Bulldog
- Bull Mastiff
- Dachshund
- Great Dane
- Saint Bernard

## Barkers and Yappers

All dogs bark after a fashion—except those that have had their voice boxes removed—and there is a nice, hot place in the hereafter for anyone who does that to a dog. A perfect example of throwing money at a problem instead of investing the time to correct the problem. We have client dogs whose former owners de-barked them. And you know what? They still try to bark and they make the most irritating noise, like barking seals. And they do it incessantly.

Granted, some dogs bark more than others. Basenjis are barkless, but they too make a funny little noise. Golden Retrievers just kind of woof, if they can muster up the energy. The Maltese and the Yorkie have deservedly bad reps as yappers. In Chapter Eight we deal with chronic barkers and other behavioral problems.

## But I'm Allergic to Dogs . . .

If you've dismissed the idea of getting a puppy because you are allergic to dogs, it could be that you are allergic only to certain breeds. If you choose a low-dander dog, you may be able to have a puppy and avoid all that sniffling and sneezing.

Poodles don't shed and—here's a bonus—they come in three sizes. Wheaten Terriers are almost shed-free because they have hair instead of fur, but they should be hand-stripped to keep their coats looking good. That means that every three or four months you will need to take a special instrument called a stripping knife and pluck out every dead hair, a somewhat tedious process. Cairn Terriers and Bichon Frises are also low-dander dogs that are almost shed-free. All make wonderful pets for the allergy-prone.

## Kritter Sitters' Top Ten Breeds

We work closely with the following breeds and have the opportunity to observe their behavior on a daily basis. Our Top Ten were chosen for two reasons: They have great dispositions and most are wonderful with children. Most can adapt to smaller living spaces, although the Golden Retriever does need a place to run. Our picks, not in order of preference:

1. **Labrador Retriever**. Sociable, outgoing, friendly, good with kids, good-natured, easy to train. Gentle and loyal, a perfect family pet. Does require lots of exercise. Downside: prone to hip dysplasia (genetic degeneration of the joint) and cataracts. Lives only 10 to 12 years. Average adult weight: 55 to 75 pounds.

2. **Border Collie**. Intelligent, cooperative, a joy to be around. High energy, almost frenetic. Good with kids, loves to play ball or fetch a Frisbee. Quick learner. Great watchdog. Downside: Must be kept busy or will drive you crazy. Average adult weight: 35 to 50 pounds.

3. **Australian Shepherd**. Smart, obedient, energetic, clownish. Good with kids. Downside: high maintenance. Needs a large yard, lots of exercise. Prone to hip dysplasia. Average adult weight: 45 to 65 pounds.

4. **Rottweiler**. Brave, intelligent, alert, formidable. Potential for behavioral problems if not well socialized. Great watchdog. Good with kids. Downside: Likes to be top dog, abhors competition for the family's affections, and may decide one day to have your rabbit for dinner. Average adult weight: 80 to 135 pounds.

5. **Great Dane**. Gentle, loyal, affectionate, regal. Responds well to training. Low energy—no jogging, please. Needs daily outdoor exercise, but can live in a small space. Downside: May eat you out of house and home, has life expectancy of only 10 to 12 years. Average adult weight: 120 to 160 pounds.

6. **Pug**. Playful, affectionate, good with kids, covets attention. Doesn't breathe well and is not big on exercise. Somewhat stubborn. Downside: If face folds are not kept meticulously clean, they smell awful and may become infected. Unless you're as rich as the late, Pug-loving Duchess of Windsor, who had a staff to handle such dis-

tasteful matters, daily wrinkle swabbing is a fact of life. Sheds a lot. Average adult weight: 14 to 18 pounds.

7. **Maltese.** Gentle but hardy. A sweet little lapdog with charm plus. Basically a couch potato and a pillow princess. Downside: prone to knee problems. Fair-skinned and allergy-prone. White fur requires frequent bathing and grooming. Average adult weight: 4 to 6 pounds.

8. **Poodle,** all sizes. Standards are highly intelligent. Clever, fun to be around, endearing, sociable, adaptable, and quick to learn. Downside: Need frequent grooming, especially if you like those pom-poms. Prone to patellar dislocation (slipping kneecap). Average adult weights: 5 to 7 pounds (Toy), 14 to 17 pounds (Miniature), 45 to 60 pounds (Standard).

9. **Golden Retriever.** Intelligent, affectionate, eager to please. The perfect dog for an outdoor-oriented family. People just have to smile when they see these big, floppy dogs. Downside: prone to hip and elbow dysplasia and cataracts. Lives only 10 to 12 years. Average adult weight: 55 to 80 pounds.

10. **Greater Swiss Mountain Dog.** Regal, loving, smart, handsome, great with children. Great dog for first-time dog owners. Good jogger. Downside: prone to hip and elbow dysplasia, bloat, and eye problems. Can't take hot climes. Needs a large yard. Average adult weight: 75 to 115 pounds.

# Our Second Ten

Some of the dogs on this list are a little hyper and can be snappy with children.

Although they didn't quite make the cut for our Top Ten list, these dogs make wonderful pets if properly trained and socialized:

1. **German Shepherd.** Fearless, devoted, intelligent, loyal, quick to learn. Aggressive only if trained to be. Great watchdog. Good family dog, good

with kids. Basically just an oversized lapdog. Wash-and-wear. Downside: prone to hip dysplasia. Average adult weight: 70 to 95 pounds.

2. **Briard.** Kind, reliable, intelligent, independent. Downside: slightly difficult to train. Can be aggressive toward other dogs. Prone to hip dysplasia and to progressive retinal atrophy leading to severe loss of vision. Average adult weight: 60 to 90 pounds.

3. **Old English Sheepdog.** Playful, intelligent, loyal. Good with kids, strangers, other pets. Downside: prone to hip dysplasia and to progressive retinal atrophy. Can be hard to train. Requires frequent grooming. Average adult weight: 90 to 100 pounds.

4. **Cairn Terrier.** Clownish, smart, hardy, fearless. Personality plus, a great companion. A sweet little "I want to be with you" lapdog—with a stubborn streak. Downside: May like to dig and bark. Prone to patellar dislocation. Average adult weight: 13 to 16 pounds.

5. **West Highland Terrier.** Spirited, bright, affectionate, good-natured. Downside: Needs frequent bathing and grooming. Tends to be a little barky. Average adult weight: 15 to 19 pounds.

6. **English Bulldog.** Gentle, calm, reliable disposition. Personality plus, very loving. Not a dog to jog with. Downside: prone to Cherry Eye, a growth at inside corner of the eye, and to infections in the face folds. Average adult weight: 40 to 50 pounds.

7. **Schnauzer.** All sizes. Whimsical, clownish, good watchdog. Standard is easy to train; Giant and Miniature are somewhat stubborn. All but the Giant breed can be yappers. Downside: Needs frequent grooming. Average adult weight: 13 to 17 pounds (Miniature), 30 to 50 pounds (Standard), 70 to 90 pounds (Giant).

8. **Airedale Terrier.** Lively, loyal, reliable, fun. Easy to train. Does well with older children. Okay with strangers. Downside: Can be aggressive toward other dogs, including a second dog introduced into household. Requires frequent grooming. Average adult weight: 50 to 75 pounds.

9. **Bearded Collie.** Good family dog. Very clean, a good choice for people with allergies. Easy to train. Likes lots of exercise time outside.

Downside: high maintenance, requires frequent grooming. Average adult weight: 45 to 60 pounds.

10. **Jack Russell Terrier.** Curious, intelligent, energetic, vigilant, athletic. Downside: prone to congenital dwarfism. (A good breeder is very important.) Needs lots of exercise. Hyper and likes to bark. Difficult to train. Aggressive toward other dogs. Average adult weight: 12 to 15 pounds.

# From Toy to Giant: 147 Choices

If you want a purebred dog, you have 147 choices—and those are just the breeds recognized by the American Kennel Club (AKC). (Worldwide, there are hundreds more.) The AKC-anointed breeds range in size from the Toys, such as Chihuahuas, Malteses, and Miniature Dachshunds—dogs that stand less than a foot tall—to the Giant breeds, such as the Great Danes, Saint Bernards, and Great Pyrenees—which may stand more than three feet tall. We list some of the dogs within breeds separately by size.

Typically, the tiny dogs are about nine inches tall and weigh less than ten pounds fully grown. Next up the scale are the small breeds, such as Jack Russells and Beagles, which may be a foot tall and weigh up to 90 pounds. Extra-large dogs, such as Great Danes and Saint Bernards, will average more than two feet in height and may weigh up to 100 pounds. Now, let's take a look at all of the AKC-sanctioned breeds.

The AKC divides the breeds into seven groups—Working Dogs, Herding Dogs, Sporting Dogs, Hounds, Terriers, Toys, and, finally, Non-Sporting, which includes an unlikely mix of breeds that just don't fit anywhere else. This explains why at a dog show you may see a Miniature Poodle competing for best-of-group honors with a Chow Chow.

Now, let's take a look at the groups.

# The Canine Workaholics

Dogs in this group were bred to protect property, pull sleds, or perform water rescues. Although they make intelligent, loyal companions, their size and strength must be taken into consideration when choosing a family pet. Powerful dogs, such as the heavy-coated Malamutes, Samoyeds, and Huskies, all need plenty of exercise. They tend to be strong-willed and can be difficult to train. And these dogs are not likely to take to living in the tropics.

The guard/protection dogs—including the Akita, Rottweiler, Great Pyrenees, Boxer, Doberman Pinscher, and Schnauzer—are highly intelligent, loyal, and quick to learn, and they make good companions, but because of their aggressive and territorial tendencies, they must be properly trained and socialized from puppyhood. The rescue dogs, such as the Newfoundland and the Saint Bernard, are large animals with dense coats and they, too, prefer cool climes. They are very intelligent, and can be wonderful pets and great with kids, if dog and child are brought up together. Their considerable heft alone makes them unsuitable as pets for some families. As the name implies, all of the dogs listed below were bred to work, and they retain a strong work ethic. They love being useful and focused on a task and, without firm direction, can be hard to handle.

### THE WORKING DOGS

- Akita
- Alaskan Malamute
- Anatolian Shepherd
- Bernese Mountain Dog
- Boxer
- Bullmastiff
- Doberman Pinscher
- Komondor
- Kuvasz (Don't ask. We've never seen one, either.)
- Mastiff
- Newfoundland
- Portuguese Water Dog
- Rottweiler

- Giant Schnauzer
- Great Dane
- Greater Swiss Mountain Dog
- Great Pyrenees

- Saint Bernard
- Samoyed
- Siberian Husky
- Standard Schnauzer

# Born to Herd

While you could probably live a lifetime without encountering a Belgian Tervuren, many of the other herding dogs are very popular pets. Some dogs in this group, such as the Border Collie, German Shepherd, and Old English Sheepdog, were bred originally to herd cattle or sheep. Others, including the Australian Cattle Dog, the Bouvier des Flandres, and the low-slung Corgis, were bred to drive cattle or sheep long distances. The Corgis can move a herd of cattle to pasture just by nipping at the bovines' heels, although it's unlikely that you will choose this breed for that trait.

The herding dogs are loyal, great with kids—although they do sometimes mistake them for creatures to be herded—and they tend to stick close to home. But expect to spend lots of time throwing things so they can retrieve. They want to please you by working, whether that's penning sheep or fetching a Frisbee. And they are easily trained. These dogs will never sit at your feet while you relax with a glass of wine, unlike a Retriever, which will play ball for a while and then happily lie down beside you. The driving dogs are natural athletes and have an aggression gene that must be socialized out of them when they are pups.

## THE HERDING DOGS

- Australian Cattle Dog
- Australian Shepherd
- Bearded Collie
- Belgian Malinois
- Belgian Sheepdog
- Belgian Tervuren
- Border Collie
- Bouvier des Flandres
- Briard
- Canaan Dog
- Collie (Rough- and Smooth-Coated)
- German Shepherd
- Old English Sheepdog
- Polish Lowland Sheepdogs
- Puli
- Shetland Sheepdog
- Welsh Corgi (Cardigan) and Welsh Corgi (Pembroke)

# The Canine Jocks

Both the Pointers and the Retrievers were bred originally to help their masters flush out and retrieve birds—and they still love to run and fetch. The Pointers are high-energy dogs that need plenty of exercise and enough land on which to indulge their run-and-fetch instincts. The Retrievers are friendly, loyal, and laid-back, and make great family pets, but do like lots of attention. The Spaniels, also bred as bird hunters, are child-friendly and loyal, but can drive you crazy with their whining if they feel left out. They're also a bit naughty and will eat anything that doesn't eat them first, including your shoes. We've seen table legs literally reduced by inches by a gnawing Cocker. If all else fails, the Spaniels will chew their paws—sometimes out of boredom, sometimes because they've been left alone and they're anxious.

## THE SPORTING DOGS

- American Water Spaniel
- Brittany
- Chesapeake Bay Retriever
- Clumber Spaniel
- Cocker Spaniel
- Curly-coated Retriever
- English Cocker Spaniel
- English Setter
- English Springer Spaniel
- Field Spaniel
- Flat-Coated Retriever
- German Shorthaired Pointer
- German Wirehaired Pointer
- Golden Retriever
- Gordon Setter
- Irish Setter
- Irish Water Spaniel
- Labrador Retriever
- Pointer
- Spinone Italiano
- Sussex Spaniel
- Vizsla
- Weimaraner
- Welsh Springer Spaniel
- Wirehaired Pointing Griffon

# Nothin' but a Hound Dog

This is a wildly disparate group (picture the Afghan and the Dachshund, very strange bedfellows indeed), but all of these breeds were originally small-game hunters. The Sighthounds, which include the Afghan, the Borzoi, and the Basenji, are great sprinters, always just waiting for an opportunity to be off-leash—and away they go. The Scenthounds, which include the Basset, the Beagle, and the Bloodhound, are perpetually sniffing around and are apt to take off if they smell something more interesting than you. They all have the appetite of a starving hyena. All hound dogs love to run, have a well-developed sense of curiosity, and—yes—in many ways "ain't nothin' but a hound dog." Some hounds will bay at the moon—and most people don't really want a dog that's going to be out there howling away.

Finally, there are the large-game hounds, such as the Norwegian

Elkhound and the Rhodesian Ridgeback. Originally bred to hunt lions, they are physically powerful, strong-willed, and plucky, and require lots of exercise. But they make devoted and loyal pets.

## THE HOUNDS

- Afghan Hound (possibly the most elegant of dogs, frequently seen posing majestically for photographs in slick home-design magazines or in advertisements for fancy cars)
- Basenji
- Basset Hound
- Beagle
- Black-and-Tan Coonhound
- Bloodhound
- Borzoi (another very aristocratic breed)
- Dachshund
- Foxhound (American)
- Foxhound (English)
- Greyhound
- Harrier
- Ibizan Hound
- Irish Wolfhound
- Norwegian Elkhound
- Otterhound
- Petit Basset Griffon Vendeen
- Pharaoh Hound
- Plott Hound
- Rhodesian Ridgeback
- Saluki
- Scottish Deerhound
- Whippet

# Terriers: Decidedly Type A

One group of terriers, which includes the Airedale, Bedlington, Cairn, and West Highland Terriers, was bred specifically to rid farms of foxes, rats, and other rodents. Unfortunately, the digging gene is still very pronounced, and these dogs will dig determinedly in your backyard, yapping happily the whole time. They are also playful and seemingly never low on energy. Another Terrier group, which includes the Bull and Staffordshire Bull Terriers, was bred either to fight dogs or to bait bulls—and these breeds remain somewhat pugnacious. They can be dangerous unless properly trained. (The Pit Bull, which has such a bad reputation, is not an AKC-recognized breed.) "Determined" is the word that pops into mind when describing the Terriers. They tend to be clownish, and never boring, but having a Terrier is a little like having three or four toddlers loose in the house. Untrained or left alone, they will become barkers, chewers, and urination markers. Terriers as a whole have little patience with other dogs or pets.

### THE TERRIERS

- Airedale Terrier
- American Staffordshire Terrier
- Australian Terrier
- Bedlington Terrier
- Border Terrier
- Bull Terrier
- Cairn Terrier (the most famous example of which is Toto in *The Wizard of Oz*)
- Dandie Dinmont Terrier
- Fox Terrier (Smooth)
- Fox Terrier (Wire)
- German Pinscher
- Irish Terrier
- Jack Russell Terrier
- Kerry Blue Terrier
- Lakeland Terrier
- Manchester Terrier (Standard)
- Miniature Bull Terrier
- Miniature Schnauzer
- Norfolk Terrier
- Norwich Terrier
- Scottish Terrier
- Sealyham Terrier
- Skye Terrier
- Soft-Coated Wheaten Terrier
- Staffordshire Bull Terrier
- Welsh Terrier
- West Highland White Terrier

## Small and Snooty

These winsome charmers are the pillow princesses. Bred originally as companions for royalty, they love—indeed, expect—to be pampered. What they excel at is being adorable. Aside from a tendency to be a bit yappy, they are a good choice for apartment dwellers, as they are both small in size and think that jumping onto your lap is just about enough exercise for one day. But untrained they can be holy terrors. Pugs aren't for kids—those cute little smushed-in noses make it hard for them to breathe and they wear out easily. Other Toy breeds are simply not hardy enough for child's play. A Pekingese can break a leg just jumping off a couch, and the Italian Greyhound's spindly bones are alarmingly fragile.

### THE TOYS

- Affenpinscher
- Brussels Griffon (that little scene-stealer that won over Jack Nicholson in *As Good As It Gets*)
- Cavalier King Charles Spaniel
- Chihuahua (which, thanks to those Taco Bell commercials, has enjoyed a surge in popularity)
- Chinese Crested
- English Toy Spaniel
- Havanese
- Italian Greyhound
- Japanese Chin
- Maltese
- Manchester Terrier
- Miniature Pinscher
- Papillon
- Pekingese
- Pomeranian
- Poodle
- Pug
- Shih Tzu
- Silky Terrier
- Toy Fox Terrier
- Yorkshire Terrier

# And All the Rest . . .

These breeds are a mixed bag, with very different traits. The Chow Chow may look like a teddy bear, and can be a wonderful pet, but is known to be fiercely loyal to his closest human companion and downright unfriendly to strangers. A friend on the East Coast told us of coming home one winter day to find that a furnace repairman had been trapped in the basement for hours, as her black Chow, Loong, stood at the top of the stairs, growling ominously. Naturally aggressive, Chows can be trained to be good guard dogs. Bulldogs were bred to fight bulls, but, although they look quite ferocious, they have evolved into gentle, loving creatures and are terrific with children.

## NON-SPORTING DOGS

- American Eskimo Dog
- Bichon Frise
- Boston Terrier
- Bulldog
- Chinese Shar-pei
- Chow Chow
- Dalmatian
- Finnish Spitz
- French Bulldog
- Keeshond
- Lhasa Apso
- Löwchen
- Poodle
- Schipperke
- Shiba Inu
- Tibetan Spaniel
- Tibetan Terrier

# The Ten Breeds Most Likely to Run Up Your Vet Bill

1. **English Bulldog**: breathing problems, skin problems, lameness
2. **Cocker Spaniel**: ear, skin, and eye problems
3. **Shar-pei**: skin problems, digestion difficulties
4. **Chow Chow**: skin problems, digestion problems
5. **German Shepherd**: eye and skin problems, lameness, gastrointestinal difficulties
6. **Boxer**: skin problems, heart ailments, gastrointestinal difficulties
7. **Dalmatian**: skin problems, urinary tract disorders, deafness. Popularity has proved disastrous to Dalmatians, with puppy mills upping the supply to meet demand, resulting in a physically weakened breed.

8. **West Highland Terrier**: skin problems
9. **Doberman Pinscher**: heart ailments, prostate problems, skin problems
10. **Collie**: blindness

Vet bills are a big consideration when deciding on a breed. Any of the heavy-coated, heavy-eared dogs, such as Poodles and English Spaniels, are susceptible to ear infections because not enough air circulates in there and bacteria breed like mad. With Poodles, kidney and urinary tract infections are a problem. Golden Retrievers and German Shepherds are prone to hip dysplasia, but a reputable breeder will certify that a puppy has not inherited this defect. We had a client who bought a beautiful Golden Retriever, only to have to have the pup's hips replaced before she was six months old.

## Unhappy Surprises

If you're thinking about getting someone a puppy as a surprise, think again. If it's to be a gift for a child, a much better idea is to give the child a picture of a puppy of the breed, and then have the child go with you to pick out her dog. Dog and child will have a chance to get acquainted in the dog's own place, where he doesn't feel scared and anxious, rather than in a strange house.

Actually, it's a terrible idea to give anyone a puppy as a surprise. You may think that your mother, who lives alone, should have a furry companion when, in reality, that's the last thing she wants. She may be counting her blessings that she no longer has children at home or other living things to take care of. Too often, these well-intended surprises wind up at the nearest animal shelter.

# 2

# Picking
# the Perfect Pup

Chances are that you're just looking for a nice pet, not a show dog that will bring home blue ribbons by the bushel. So, the all-important question is: purebred or mutt?

There are arguments for buying a purebred. For one thing, if you buy a Borzoi, you know your pup's going to grow up to look like a Borzoi and not a Bulldog—or some bizarre Dachshund-Dalmatian mix. You also know within a few inches and a few pounds how large he's going to be full grown. Finally, you know—at least statistically—what his disposition is likely to be and whether he's apt to be a good watchdog, good with kids, or whatever.

However, a purebred is going to cost more, and is more likely to be stolen. Purebred dogs also tend to have more medical problems, a result of the inbreeding of lines to produce dogs deemed by humans to be perfect specimens—dogs that will win those ribbons.

## The Case for Mutts

Mutts—or to be more politically correct, mixed-breed dogs—tend to be healthier because of their gene mix. Dad's apt to be a chap that Mom met on the street. One of our favorite dogs was a wispy mongrel with hair sticking up all over his head, hair sprouting from his nose, hair everywhere—one of the most endearing animals we've ever seen. We don't think that AKC is necessarily better than Heinz 57 Varieties. However, mixed-breed dogs have unpredictable temperaments and tend to be more difficult to train. It's a crapshoot. By buying or adopting a mixed-breed dog or a pound puppy, you will be making a small contribution toward reducing pet overpopulation and, quite likely, will be saving a dog's life.

If your heart is set on a purebred, and you've settled on a breed, we're going to tell you how to find a reputable breeder. One caveat: If you aren't sure whether you want a Cocker Spaniel or a Shar-pei or a Dachshund, and you plan to visit a number of breeders before deciding, never, ever take your children with you. They'll want the first dog they see. Then you'll go to the next breeder and they'll want that dog. You could wind up with either a dozen dogs or an irreconcilable child. But, once you have settled on a breed and a breeder, you should take the kids along to help choose from the litter.

Now, the second big decision: where to buy your puppy.

## Pet Store Puppies: Just Say No

At any major shopping mall from coast to coast, you're apt to find The Gap or Victoria's Secret and an upscale pet shop. Typically, there will be a few adorable puppies in the window and, outside, an appreciative knot of lookie-loos "ooh-ing" and "aah-ing." Elbowing their way to the front, these shoppers melt like jelly as the pups do what they do best, which is to look irresistible.

Those who venture inside find a dozen or more equally enchanting puppies peeking out at them from their cages, heads cocked just so, tails wagging, all but begging to be taken home. The pet shop is counting on people like you to be unable to resist, especially when the oh-so-helpful store employees suggest that perhaps you'd like to hold one of the puppies. Their mission in life is to send you home with an item not on your shopping list—a puppy. But puppies should never be impulse buys.

### DID YOU KNOW?

Did you know that a puppy is capable of learning, and of making conscious decisions, when he is only three weeks old?

# Puppy Mills: A Horror Story

That's not the only reason for passing up pet store puppies. Virtually all of the chain pet stores buy their puppies from brokers who buy them from the infamous puppy mills that operate mainly in Kansas, Missouri, Iowa, Nebraska, Pennsylvania, Oklahoma, and Arkansas. If you buy a puppy mill dog, you are not only setting yourself up for heartache, but are subsidizing an inhumane industry with a single mission: breeding puppies for profit as fast as they can, and hang the consequences to you or the dog. The American Society for the Prevention of Cruelty to Animals (ASPCA) and the Humane Society of the United States estimate that nine of ten pet store puppies are products of puppy mills. And, the Humane Society puts puppy sales at pet stores at $500,000 a year.

These puppy factories—there are at least four thousand in the United States—have been exposed and castigated in numerous newspaper and magazine articles and in investigative reports on television. However, despite well-documented horror stories, they continue to flourish, mostly through sales to pet stores. The horror stories include overbreeding of brood bitches, starting at six months of age and continuing in every heat cycle (every sixty-six days!) until, worn out at the age of about five, the poor bitches are unceremoniously disposed of. (Yes, put to death.)

Overbreeding is only one of the unconscionable practices at these horrible places. There are puppies with oozing sores, puppies sharing their maggot-infested food with rats. Adult dogs may spend their entire lives in filthy, cramped wire cages stacked one atop another, wallowing in their own waste. They likely have never nibbled a blade of grass or chased a ball, slept on a soft bed, or been cuddled in a soft lap. Because a puppy's cuteness factor peaks at between seven and ten weeks, these pups are ripped away from their mothers as young as four weeks, crammed in crates, and trucked or flown to pet stores or to brokers, who, in turn, sell them to the stores.

Not only are these puppies at high risk for health problems, but because they have never been socialized they are apt to be destructive or aggressive. The miserable lives of their dams are not conducive to making them loving mothers. So, never having experienced maternal bonding, the pups may be nippy and unpredictable. Having been allowed to relieve themselves wherever they wished, or forced to eliminate where they slept and ate, they can be very difficult to housebreak.

## The Paper Trail: No Guarantee

If you're not yet warned away from pet store pups, consider this: That "purebred" puppy with the whopping $500 price tag may not even be a purebred. Mill operators run loose operations that allow for mix-ups. But, you say, the puppies are AKC-registered. AKC registry is not a guarantee of a healthy dog. The pup's parents may be purebreds, but pretty dreadful specimens, or they may have genetic defects that they passed along to the pup. And, because the AKC registry operates on an honor system, mill operators have been known to cheat, falsely reporting the size of a litter so as to obtain extra registration slips for puppies of questionable lineage. The only way to guarantee what you're getting is to buy from an ethical breeder.

When you buy that pricey pet store puppy, you are subsidizing these Simon Legrees of the dog world. At the same time, you are helping to ensure that thousands of hapless dogs will continue to live in abject misery.

Why doesn't somebody shut these places down? Although an Animal Welfare Act was enacted in 1966, cruelty to dogs continues largely because of spotty enforcement by the U.S. Department of Agriculture, which is charged with inspection of puppy mills. Thirteen states have enacted "lemon laws" to protect puppy buyers. These laws give buyers redress (refunds or reimbursement for veterinary bills), but they do nothing to help the poor dogs suffering in the puppy mills.

If, despite everything, you insist on buying a pet store puppy, at least protect yourself by asking these vital questions:

✔ Where did these puppies come from? (Ask to see the documents. An AKC or United Kennel Club registration guarantees nothing about the dog, but does tell you that the kennel has not lost its registration privileges because of questionable conditions or fraud.)
✔ Can I get a copy of the breeder's certification of health, including x-raying of hips for dysplasia and inspection of eyes for disease?
✔ What are the health problems common to the breed?
✔ What is the breed's temperament?
✔ How much exercise will this dog need? How much grooming? Is he by nature a barker? (You'll be lucky if the store staff can do much more than suggest you buy a breed book.)

If the pet store can't give you the answers, or refuses to share vital information with you, walk away.

Yes, there have been good puppies that have come out of pet stores, but the odds are very much against it. A more typical scenario: You take the puppy home and, within days or weeks, the dog develops health problems. So, you take him back to the store, hoping for advice or maybe a refund. Of course, that friendly clerk who sold you the puppy knows little or nothing about the breed or about dog health in general. Or, your puppy may be wee-weeing all over your floor and, in desperation, you phone the pet store. You're kidding yourself if you think you're going to get help. The store has processed your credit card and now you're on your own. Even if you have a contract, you're not likely to get a cash refund when you return a sick puppy. You're more apt to get a credit—entitling you to choose another problem puppy. And guess what? The store will probably turn right around and sell the returned puppy to another unsuspecting customer.

# Finding a Good Breeder

There are breeders, and there are breeders. There are disreputable breeders who advertise on the Internet, eager to ship you a puppy sight unseen. They don't give a hoot whether you'll be a responsible dog owner, so long as your credit card isn't refused. There are backyard breeders, who may breed their bitch to pick up a little pocket money at Christmas or to recoup their investment. You're better off buying from one of them than from a pet store because you will at least have a chance to see the mother dog and the conditions under which the puppy was bred. But the backyard breeder may not know much about the dam or sire or if she or he had been tested for potential health problems. Because these breeders tend to breed the most popular dogs, such as Labs, Golden Retrievers, and German Shepherds, they are perpetuating—either through ignorance or casual breeding practices—a line of dogs with genetic defects. And you're apt to pay just as much for your puppy as if you bought him from a reputable breeder. Some pet stores buy locally from these backyard breeders, another reason to veto a pet store puppy.

So where do you find a reputable breeder?

There is no national registry that rates dog breeders on the basis of their ethics or the quality of their pups, and in most states breeders do not need to be licensed, so it's up to you to do most of the sleuthing.

It's worth the effort. You are making an emotional commitment to this puppy, as well as a financial one. (Out-of-pocket expenses over the first year of a puppy's life average $600.) Veterinarians frequently have names of reputable breeders, as do dog groomers. You'll find listings of reputable breeders in the *Breeders' Journal*, available at many pet stores. (Top breeders rely on their reputations and do not have to place newspaper ads to sell their puppies.) The AKC's Breeder Referral Hotline is an automated service that will put you in touch with a breeder representative in your area. Breed clubs on the Internet will refer you to good breeders. Just go to any of the major search engines, type in "dog," and you'll be inundated with links to breeds. Another good way to find a breeder is by going to AKC-sanctioned dog shows, where many of these breeders compete.

Good breeders generally have a long history with the breed, have studied the breed, know the breed standard, and are committed to doing their part to make the breed stronger. They are not in the business of turning out assembly line puppies. They actually care what happens to you and your puppy after your check clears. Good breeders will be looking you over, just as you are looking them over. They want their puppies to go to good homes, where they will be loved and well cared for. These breeders know the traits of their breed and whether their puppies will fit your lifestyle. They won't lead you to believe that their breed is without doggie faults, and they will be open in discussing with you behavior problems and/or health problems specific to the breed.

A good breeder will know the litter, which are the dominant puppies, which the shy ones, and will be able to advise which one will be best for you. A good breeder will have socialized the pups, played with them, made them members of the family.

# Quizzing the Breeder

Here's what you'll want to ask before buying a pup:

- ✔ Are the sire and dam AKC-registered? Does the pup have AKC papers?
- ✔ Do you have a pedigree chart for the pup, and may I see it? (This chart is a sort of doggie genealogy, often going back three or more generations. If the pup is descended from canine bluebloods, he may have more potential. And he may be more valuable.)
- ✔ How long have you been raising dogs? Raising this breed?
- ✔ What—good and bad—should I know about the breed?
- ✔ May I see the dam and the sire? (Yes, puppies do take after their parents.)
- ✔ Were the pup's parents x-rayed to rule out hip dysplasia? (This hip dislocation is prevalent among large breeds. Ask to see a certificate from the Orthopedic Foundation of America.) Ask about the pup's general health and ask to see the inoculation record and evidence of worming. Most good breeders will give you a year's guarantee that the pup is free of genetic defects.
- ✔ Do you breed more than one breed of dog? (If the answer is yes, this is a red flag. A little learning about a breed is a dangerous thing. There's even the possibility that the breeder might not know who sired whom.)
- ✔ May I look around your facilities? (You'll be checking for clean, humane conditions. Are the dogs in good physical shape? Do they seem happy? Is the kennel free of "bathroom" smells? Is there an exercise area? Do the dogs have a proper place to sleep?)
- ✔ What are your conditions of sale? Will you take back a puppy that does not work out? Some breeders not only will take the pup back, but will insist that you offer the dog to them first

should you for any reason not be able to keep him. This is a very good sign. If he were not a good dog, the breeder would be happy to be rid of him. Other breeders have a spay-neuter clause in their contracts. This too is a sign of a responsible breeder and should not present a problem for you except in the unlikely event that you plan to raise a show dog with lucrative breeding potential. You and the breeder should go over the contract together, point by point.

✔ Do you belong to a local or national breed club?

✔ May I have the names and telephone numbers of people to whom you've sold puppies? If the breeder cannot, or will not, give you referrals, this is reason enough to seek another breeder. What is this breeder afraid you'll find out?

Every litter has not so good, good, better, and best. The best are those genetically destined to become show dogs, and you will pay accordingly. The others are labeled "pet quality," which for most people is just fine. This is not an indication that there's anything really wrong with the dog. He may simply be a little long in the snout or have a less-than-perfect bite. An ethical breeder will tell you which pups are "pet quality."

# Buyer Beware

Beware of breeders who:

✔ Have changed the name of the kennel. This breeder may be inbreeding dogs like crazy for quick profit, then moving on. One week it's the J and J Kennel, the next week the M and M Kennel.

✔ Won't give you the name of their veterinarian. Some disreputable breeders save money by doing their own vaccinating.

You can bet that their dogs have not been checked for genetic defects.

✔ Are new to this breeding business. If there is no paper trail, you cannot learn anything about a pup's ancestry. Yes, every breeder must start somewhere, but the most reputable breeders intern under established breeders, who will be able to vouch for them.

✔ Breed their dogs too often. Breeding a dam heat to heat makes for a sick mother dog and unhealthy puppies. A good breeder alternates the bitches year to year.

✔ Have dogs on the property that are either unfriendly or don't interact with the breeder.

✔ Keep a number of dogs of different breeds on the premises. (Accidents do happen.)

✔ Keep their dogs outside, with little human contact.

✔ Offer to let you take the puppy home at six weeks of age. We like to see a puppy stay with the mother for at least eight, and preferably twelve, weeks. She teaches her pups manners, pecking order, and independence.

✔ Won't give you an unconditional guarantee that the puppy is healthy.

✔ Won't tell you anything negative about the breed. You should be told, for example, that those cute, fuzzy Akita pups may grow up to be very aggressive little devils.

## What About Pound Puppies?

Should you decide to rescue a puppy from a shelter, don't give the shelter dogs a quick once-over and decide, "I want that cute black one." You will want to interact with the dog, see how he reacts to being handled. At best, a shelter is a stressful environment for any animal. A dog that doesn't come forward, eager to meet and please you, may not be unfriendly, he may just be frightened or depressed or stressed out. On the other hand, the puppy that all but screams, "Over here! Take me!" may be a bit too rambunctious once you get him home. Shelters are not apt to know much about their dogs' histories—many of these pups were simply abandoned—so adopting a shelter dog is a little like buying a used car. You may be inheriting someone else's problems. Most of these dogs have been given up because their owners didn't know how to handle behavior problems that they themselves might have caused. Instead of working to solve the problems, they just dumped the dogs. We have a few choice words for those people.

Getting an aggressive dog like a Rottweiler from a shelter is an iffy proposition. That dog may have been abused and, if so, he won't have forgotten. The first time your child reaches out to pet him, he might try to rip her arm off.

You may not a want a shelter pup the first time around, but when people want a second dog, we do encourage them to get a pound puppy and save a life. There are lots of pound puppies that just aren't wanted anymore (often it's because the owners failed to research the breed before they leaped). Many of these are beautiful dogs that never did anything wrong. Nevertheless, they will be put to sleep if not claimed within days.

Taking in a stray is another matter. If you find a stray puppy not wearing tags, and you have scoured the neighborhood without luck to see if someone has posted a "lost dog" sign, you should first turn the dog in to the local branch of the ASPCA. This is where a distraught owner will look first. You don't want just to take the puppy in—there may be a heartbroken owner out there somewhere. The pup will be held by the ASPCA for ten days. At the end of that period, you will be allowed to adopt the dog if he is unclaimed. If you do adopt him, take him right away to a vet to find out how well he's been cared for. If the puppy's been abused, you may be setting yourself up for behavioral problems. Just taking in a lost puppy and claiming him as your own is not right.

For people on limited incomes who cannot pay hundreds of dollars for a purebred puppy, the local animal shelter is the safest and most economical source. The AKC estimates that one in four dogs in shelters is a purebred. Shelter dogs have had their shots and, if old enough, have been spayed or neutered before being placed for adoption. If you adopt a pound puppy, you must be patient. The pup will need time to adjust to his new environment and may have been traumatized by the shelter experience. A dog's life in a shelter is not a happy one, with the constant cacophony of barking, confinement in small spaces, and minimal human attention.

## Rescue Me

All of our dogs with the exception of Mr. Murphy, our Toy Poodle, have been rescue dogs. What each of them has taught us is that, by going that extra mile, you will be rewarded a thousand times over.

Rescue dogs are not pound puppies. They are purebreds that for some reason have been given up by their families. Rescue organizations abound. Every AKC-registered breed has one or more rescue groups that take in dogs and care for them until new homes can be found. You should be able to get rescue information on the breed that interests you from veterinarians, the ASPCA, the AKC, or from a reputable pet store (one that does not sell puppies!). As with a pound puppy, you may be unable to obtain information about the dog's history or health. But you can sleep well knowing that you aren't helping to line the pockets of some puppy mill operator.

## Hey, Look Me Over

Before signing on the dotted line, you'll want to give the pup of your choice an on-the-spot physical exam. Here's what to look for:

✔ The eyes should be clear, with no discharge or excessive tear-
ing.

✔ The coat should be shiny, with no areas of hair loss, sores, or
redness.

✔ The ears should be free of dot-sized black particles that might
indicate ear mites. If the pup shakes his head constantly, or
rubs his ears with his paws, mites might be to blame.

✔ There should be no mucous discharge from the nose. The
puppy should be able to breathe freely. Beware of a pup that's
coughing or sneezing.

✔ Do a flea check. If fleas are present, there will be tiny black
deposits the size of grains of sand in the pup's fur.

✔ Do a dental check. The pup's gums should be pink, his teeth
straight, and he should have a reasonably well-aligned bite.

✔ Diarrhea is a bad sign. Check the pup's rear end for signs of
irritation.

# 3

# Bringing
# Baby Home

**T**his may sound crazy, but the first thing you need to do in preparation for your pup's arrival is to get down on your hands and knees and crawl around your house. We call this puppy-proofing. It means checking every square inch for anything that might hurt your puppy, as well as for anything of value that your puppy might destroy.

Puppies are by nature inquisitive. They will sniff and chew everything. If a door is left open, they will dash into the street. A good rule of thumb when puppy-proofing your home is to scrutinize it just as carefully as though you were letting a toddler loose because that is, in effect, what you're doing.

## Puppy-Proofing Your Home

From floor level you're going to see all the intriguing, but dangerous, things your puppy will see, such as uncorralled electrical cords. As with toddlers, puppies' insatiable curiosity often gets them into trouble— "Oh, that looks really neat. Let me go chew on that wire plugged into that socket." It's a good idea to unplug appliances when they're not in use, and to run cords behind cabinets and affix them to the baseboard with duct tape. Unless a cord is frayed, it's safe to run it under a carpet. If you live in a carpetless house, you can anchor cords to the floor with wide strips of duct tape or you can encase those wires in hollow plastic tubing, available at hardware stores. Because puppies are smaller and more active than babies—and have sharp teeth and claws—lamp cords plugged into sockets are a real hazard and many a pup has been on the receiving end of a nasty electric shock. We place furniture strategically in front of sockets. Baby shops sell plastic gadgets that cover open sockets. And don't forget your computer. You may want to avoid a blackout by placing the computer power strip high on

## How to Puppy-Proof

**B**efore bringing your puppy home, it's essential that you make a room-by-room check for anything that might be dangerous to the dog. You'll also want to stash objects of value out of the puppy's reach. And don't forget your shoes and slippers!

Check for the following:

✔ All rooms: unprotected light sockets and unsecured electrical cords, skid-prone area rugs, miniblind cords. Also poisonous house-plants and chocolate candies
✔ Office: computer power strip, telephone cord, valuable papers
✔ Living room/den: leather-bound or other valuable books
✔ Kitchen and bathroom: toxic substances in unsecured cabinets
✔ Garden: poisonous plants, snail bait, plant insecticides
✔ Garage: antifreeze, paints and paint thinners, and other toxic products

Final check: Is your yard escape-proof, or are there fence holes or places the puppy can dig under?

a shelf, out of your puppy's reach. If your home office has no door, a baby gate can save you a lot of grief.

# Flora, Flying Objects, Flying Carpets

Knickknacks on a coffee table are irresistible to a puppy. Area rugs that aren't firmly anchored are virtual flying carpets. Puppies will rip magazines to shreds and feast on your houseplants. If you don't want plants to become puppy salad, you'll have to place them up high. Some plants commonly found in homes and gardens are highly toxic to dogs. Plant bulbs, especially daffodils, must be kept out of puppy's reach. Other common plants that are not puppy-friendly include hemlock, lupine, boxwood, clematis, ivy, columbine, bird-of-paradise, Easter lily, elephant ear, azaleas, English holly, jasmine, larkspur, lily of the valley, wisteria, delphinium, larkspur, periwinkle, buttercup, rhubarb, toadstools, spinach, and tomato vines. And, we might add, marijuana. Should you suspect poisoning, and you are unable to reach your vet, there is a twenty-four-hour help hotline, the ASPCA National Animal Control Poison Center (see Resources).

Puppies will gnaw on the legs of your tables and chairs. Spraying the furniture with Bitter Apple or Bitter Orange, available at pet stores, may deter your puppy while you are teaching him the do's and don'ts, and it won't hurt your pup or stain your carpets or upholstery. But we've found that some puppies think it's absolutely delicious.

Smart puppies will learn to open kitchen cupboards, which are apt to contain highly toxic substances. If you have the kind that can be secured by looping a rubber band around the knobs, great. If not, you may want to use baby-proofing latches, available at baby shops.

## Any Shoe in a Pinch

It's hard to remember to keep your closet doors closed. But if you don't, shoes lying on the closet floor will soon become puppy fodder. A back-of-the-door shoe rack may be the solution. You'll also need to stash your handbags out of reach. And check out your den: First editions and fine leather-bound books should be relocated to upper shelves. Your puppy will want to explore your house, and anything that is at puppy level is fair game. That includes whatever you may have stashed under the beds. Potential dangers include dryer doors left open (an invitation for the pup to curl up inside, where he may get tumble-dried with the next load of laundry) and plastic garment bags from the cleaner that can suffocate a dog. (We always tie ours in knots the minute we remove the garments and before recycling the bags.)

## Backyard Booby Traps

If you keep your trash cans in your backyard, it's wise to have the kind with snap-on safety tops to foil a curious puppy or, alternatively, to keep the cans in a locked, covered storage area. A freestanding barbecue could be tipped over by your puppy and fall on him. And you should never heat up the barbecue and leave it unattended if your puppy is in the yard. He'll waste no time investigating to see what makes coals glow.

If your puppy can get into your garage, he may get into trouble. Paint thinners and other toxic substances should be placed on high shelves. Antifreeze is deadly to dogs; by destroying the liver, it will kill them if they are not treated by a vet within twelve hours of ingesting it. It drips from beneath the car onto the driveway or the floor of the garage and, because it smells sweet, is very enticing to puppies. Containers should be wiped clean and stored on a high shelf, and rags that have been used to wipe up antifreeze should be securely wrapped and disposed of.

You'll want to secure your puppy on days when you expect someone, perhaps a meter reader or a gardener, to come into the yard. A gate left open for even a minute is too tempting. You can put the dog in a locked dog run or, if you are at home, bring him inside. And when doing your gardening, skip the toxic plant sprays and snail bait. Snail bait is deadly to dogs. If snails have taken up residence in your garden, you may want to try doing them in with either beer or salt. The safest bug killer for your plants is dishwashing detergent and water.

# Great Escapes

Is your yard escape-proof? If there's a gate leading to the street, we suggest filling the gap between gate and ground with strong wire mesh so the puppy can't dig his way out. Check your fence for holes—and make sure the fence is tall enough that the puppy can't jump right over. Because the safety of our dogs and those of our clients is all-important, our home is double-gated and double-fenced, with a chain-link fence and a ten-foot wooden fence.

If there's a way out, your puppy will find it. One of our favorite clients, Julie the Beagle, came to us with a warning from her owner that Julie was a wanderer. Not to worry, we said, Julie would be safe with us in our big fenced yard with double gates. Well, sure enough, one day we went to the movies and, when we returned home, Julie was nowhere to be found. As we were turning the house upside down in a panic, there was a knock on the front door and there stood a neighbor—holding Julie. It seems Julie had been sitting calmly on our front lawn waiting for us to find her. Baffled as to how she got out, we decided to play detective. We picked up our car keys, closed the front door, and hid behind a car across the street to spy on Julie. Not five minutes later, here she came trotting down our driveway, tail wagging in the breeze, nose to the ground. We took her back in, then repeated our little ruse, this time hiding behind a bush. Same story. Once again, we escorted her back inside and this time—feeling like idiots—we hid in the garage. Busted! Here came Julie, pushing open a bedroom window screen, then pushing up the aluminum garage door with her nose and crossing the patio to freedom. Dogs are superb at Houdini-like escapes.

# I'll Swallow It If I Can

Household cleaning products and medications that are toxic to babies are also toxic to puppies. If your new pup can manage to paw open the bathroom cabinet where you keep potentially poisonous products, he will. Again, we suggest using little plastic baby-proofing latches. Don't count on childproof pill bottles to foil the puppy; puppies have been known to chew right through them.

That box of Mrs. See's chocolates sitting on the cocktail table will be irresistible to your pup—dogs love chocolate—but there's an ingredient in dark chocolate called theobromine that in large quantities is potentially fatal to dogs. A client told of leaving her house one Christmas Eve, having wrapped the gifts and placed them under the tree. One was a five-pound box of chocolates for her father-in-law. When she returned home, her Cockapoo had ripped apart the package, eaten every chocolate (leaving the papers), and thrown up all over the other gifts. The woman was understandably hysterical, but the dog was lucky to have survived this little bit of gluttony.

You'll want to survey your house for other possible puppy booby traps, such as a table runner that can be yanked off, taking with it your precious cut-glass vase. Can your pup get himself tangled up in the cords of your miniblinds? Choke on the fringe of your Oriental carpet? If you have valuable carpets, or slip-and-slide area rugs, this might be a good time to have them cleaned and stored for a few months. Are there tight spaces in which the puppy could get wedged? Insecure moldings or exposed nails that he might pry loose?

# Puppy Hide-and-Seek

There also are things around the house that are not dangerous to the puppy, but pretty scary. If frightened, your puppy may just disappear suddenly and you'll find yourself frantically searching every cupboard and closet. The first time a puppy sees and hears a vacuum cleaner, he's certain that it is some kind of monster that devours little dogs in a single gulp and he may pull a disappearing act. On the other hand, we had a Jack Russell client named Bizet whose mission in life was to destroy every vacuum cleaner in the known universe. When we pulled ours out of the closet, her deep-rooted killer instincts arose; she leaped atop it and rode it from room to room, growling fiercely.

Mia, a client's baby "Pug from hell," a particularly mischievous pup, was awfully quiet one day. Now, when Mia was quiet, it meant trouble. Although she was the runt of the litter and about the size of a guinea pig, she was a holy terror. One of our dog sitters called and called her—no response. She looked in Mia's bed—no Mia. She began to worry: Did Murphy, her older dog, eat Mia, finally fed up with being chased around the house? Was a door left open? Did Mia, who loved to slip-slide across the hardwood floors, skid into a wall and knock herself out? Then the dog-sitter bent to pick up a pair of men's athletic shoes that our client had left by the door and something moved. There was Mia, snoozing happily in one shoe, head first, with only her tiny tail sticking out.

# Shopping for the New Puppy: The Essential Layette

Bringing your puppy home is supposed to be fun, so don't stress out. Being a first-time dog owner can be intimidating, especially if you've read some dog book that has convinced you that the pup needs a wardrobe larger than yours and the entire inventory of Toys 'R' Us.

Puppy products are a multimillion-dollar industry. You may be dazzled, and slightly overwhelmed, by the array of gizmos, bells, and whistles available at pet stores and through catalogs. There are toys that squeak, toys that rattle, and toys that bounce. There is personalized dinnerware. There are visors and bandanas, parkas trimmed with faux fur, four-legged sweatshirts and sweaters, and, for the four-legged football fan, "official" NFL doggie jerseys in authentic colors. There are bath towels with pooch's name and a pawprint logo, doggie bathtubs and electrically heated doggie beds dressed up with pawprint sheets.

Frivolities aside, it's easy to spend $250 to $500 for a cage, bowls, and the rest, depending upon where you shop—pet emporium or garage sales. If you're like us, you'll find that you can do a lot of improvising. Old blankets, for example, make fine puppy beds and are easy to wash. If you want a proper bed, you're going to get the best buys at the big discounters such as Costco, Kmart, Target, and Wal-Mart. By all means, go shopping for your puppy before bringing him home—with a list of essentials in hand that will help you to resist the luxury "extras." No matter what any salesperson may tell you, your puppy is not going to get an inferiority complex if you don't provide a Limoges water bowl (personalized) and a Victorian doggie bed with lace-trimmed armrests.

## Basic Doggie Gear

What your new puppy really needs:

- ✔ A comfortable place to sleep. This can be a big, plump pillow. If you sew, you might want to save money by making a bed from fabric scraps and stuffing it with shredded polyfoam from an arts-and-crafts store. Any strong cotton fabric, such as denim or duck, is fine. The pillow should be twice the size of your puppy and should have a zipper closing. Buttons are too easy for the pup to dislodge. To deter fleas, you might throw in a bag of cedar chips, available at any pet store. Some dog owners swear by wicker baskets, on the theory that the creaking of the wicker calms the puppy. We don't advise them for

## Collars, Leads, and Leashes

*C*ollars are largely a matter of personal taste. If you want a leather collar because you think it's very manly or very elegant, and you're willing to spend the money, get one. Or you can buy a perfectly serviceable nylon collar for pennies on the dollar.

Basically, all you need is a collar that won't come off over the pup's head and won't stretch out, because your pup's ID tags, which you must get for him before he ventures outdoors, are going to be on that collar. When you buy your dog's license, which is required in all states, you will also get a metal registration number tag that should be attached to the collar.

A good standard lead is a six- or eight-foot leather or cloth lead. For training, the six-foot length is best. Some people like chain leads because, unlike leather or nylon leads, they can't be chewed, but chains rust and can be uncomfortable in the hand. A chain lead is too heavy for a young puppy. The fifteen-foot cotton leads are great—if you live in an area where your puppy can't run out in the middle of the street while on-lead.

Extend-a-leads, the ones that zip out at the push of a button, are okay, but you have to really know what you're doing. A dog can run around you and wrap you up in the lead in a second, ripping open your leg.

In general, we don't like choke chains, but sometimes they are the only way to control a dog. They do get his attention. They should be used only when training or walking the dog, as they can snag on fences or other objects and choke the dog. Pinch or prong collars with flat-ended spikes that neither cut nor bruise the dog are effective for misbehaving dogs that have a high pain tolerance. Don't mistake these for spike collars, which are, thankfully, outlawed.

When you are ready to start training your puppy, at around four months, ask your trainer or class instructor which is the most suitable training collar.

very young dogs, as they're apt to gnaw off twigs and choke on them. A beanbag chair with a washable, removable cover is another option. Or you may want to accustom your puppy from the start to sleeping in his crate, which you'll use later to housebreak him. Hammacher Schlemmer, a company specializing in upscale "toys" for adults, and some pet catalogs sell electrically heated pet beds. At $50 to $90 a pop, we would opt for a hot-water bottle.

# The Basic Doggie Diet—And a Few Toys and Treats

**Kibble**. Good-quality (not supermarket brand) kibble formulated for puppies. Kibble is dry dog food in pellet form. To get you started, your breeder will give you some to take home, and will tell you how much to feed the puppy. Free feeding—having dry food available twenty-four hours a day—is never a good idea. The pup's gastric juices won't have time to get pumping between meals. And you don't want a fat puppy that's going to balloon into obesity. As a rule of thumb, a puppy up to twelve weeks of age should be fed four times a day. You'll want to ask your vet for advice on what kind of food—wet or dry—and what amounts are best for your pup as he grows. If you're going to be changing his diet from that given him by the breeder, it's best to do so slowly so as not to upset his stomach. You can do this by gradually mixing the new food into the old until he's weaned from the old food.

**Treats**. We like to give our dogs natural treats, such as prepared freeze-dried liver or lamb we buy at the pet store, carrots or green beans and other vegetables. Yes, puppies love raw veggies, washed but not peeled, and finely diced. If you're buying dog biscuits at the supermarket, rather than at the pet store, look for those without food coloring. The more natural the better. One of our clients always bought colored cookies for her dogs, swearing that one was partial to red, the other to green. The truth? The colors are added simply to entice you, the first-time dog owner, to buy. Your puppy doesn't care if his treats are red, green, purple, or polka-dotted. And beware of those with a "meat" coating that is supposed to look like beef. They, too, contain food coloring and will also stain your carpets. All-natural biscuits, preservative-free, are the best choice, but you'll find them only at pet stores. If you will be using treats in training your puppy, we suggest freeze-dried liver and an occasional puppy cookie. And you don't want to give your puppy a doggie cookie every time he just looks beguiling. That's like giving a child too much candy. The puppy won't be hungry at mealtime, having filled up on empty calories that can pack on pounds.

**Chews.** Your puppy is always going to be chewing something, and that something may be the leg of your Chippendale chair. To avert disaster, provide him with a good chew toy, such as a nylon bone in chicken, beef, or liver flavor. These bones are practically indestructible, last seemingly forever, and puppies love them. Real bones aren't such a good idea, as the flakes and splinters can lodge in your puppy's throat. And don't feed your dog brittle bones, such as those from chicken or pork chops or even steak, as they can splinter and split and lacerate his throat or stomach. We prefer knucklebones that have been boiled. A sterilized natural bone, available at pet stories, is okay, but be sure it is twice the width of your puppy's mouth so he can't swallow it. Compressed rawhide bones are fine, but avoid the rolled ones. They get soft, gummy, and smelly, and dogs, especially small dogs, are apt to choke on them. Years ago, when we had a horse ranch, we noticed our dogs would chew happily on the trimmings that fell to the ground when the farriers trimmed the horses' hooves. Disgusting but true. Well, horse trimmings weren't all that plentiful, but cows' hooves were, and eventually someone got the smart idea of creating rawhide bones for dogs. Kind of revolting, but dogs love them.

**Toys.** Buy five or six puppy toys and rotate them so the puppy doesn't get bored with them. If you shower him with too many toys all at once, he'll soon lose interest in all of them. Latex toys are best and should be bought with the puppy's size in mind. A Toy dog is going to get very frustrated trying to wrap his little jaws around something the size of a baseball. Buying kiddie toys at a discount toy warehouse rather than buying puppy toys at the pet store will save you money. Always check out the squeakers to make sure the puppy can't get them out and swallow them, because if he can, he will. A stomach pumping or surgery could follow. Superballs are great, as are the hard rubber Kong toys. You can stuff these with peanut butter and the puppy will be kept occupied for hours, trying to scoop out the last little bit. Puppies love Kong toys, which come in many shapes and sizes and bounce like crazy. Anything with too loud a squeak is apt to scare the pup. A big stuffed animal may be a comforting nighttime companion for your new puppy, but beware of those with eyes that the puppy might pull out and swallow.

**Bowls.** Your puppy will need two bowls, one for food, one for water. You'll want to make water available to him at all times, food only at mealtimes. You can use any suitable bowl lying around the house or buy a fancy ceramic bowl with pooch's name on it. There are bowls that store enough food and water for a pup for up to three days. We suggest that you pass on these. They are hard to keep clean, and the water tends to turn green after sitting awhile. There are molded plastic bowls in every color of the rainbow and bowls in patterns to complement your kitchen décor. We think that stainless steel bowls are best. They don't break if accidentally turned over and can be plopped in the dishwasher to be sterilized. Puppies can pick up plastic bowls and chew on them. Also, plastic bowls can get scratched, and algae and bacteria thrive in the scratches, turning the bowls green and nasty. Some puppies are even allergic to plastic. Ceramic bowls are fine, but check the bottoms to make sure they were made in the U.S.A.

# Do's and Don'ts of Feeding

- Do buy only all-natural wet or dry foods from pet stores or through pet supply catalogs. Avoid supermarket brands.
- Don't offer your puppy food that has been sitting for hours in his bowl. It may have spoiled and could cause stomach upset and diarrhea. Dispose of any wet food when he has finished eating. Dry food left in his dish should be tossed at the end of the day.
- Do make fresh water available at all times, changing it several times a day.
- Don't feed cat food to a dog. It is too high in protein and can cause bowel problems. Although it won't make your pup drop dead, eating cat food consistently will make him extremely fat. To keep your pup away from the cat's food, let the cat eat on a counter or another high place out of the pup's reach. Failing this, put the cat's dish in another room and shut the door.
- Do serve your puppy's wet food at room temperature. Cold dog food is very unappealing.
- Do watch your puppy's weight, as puppies can gain easily and it is bad for their hearts and joints. When you rub your hands down your puppy's sides, you should be able to feel his ribs.
- Do call your vet if your puppy refuses to eat for twenty-four hours. Lack of appetite could indicate serious illness.

American-made ceramics designed to hold food may not, by law, contain a lead glaze, as lead has been deemed a health hazard; those made in many other countries are not manufactured under the same restrictions. Bowls should have flat bottoms and some heft, as some puppies think tip-the-water-bowl is a great game. Whichever type of bowl you use, remember to wash it after every meal. How would you like to eat dinner off your dirty breakfast plate? If your puppy has long, floppy ears—think Bloodhound, Basset, or Setter—buy a bowl designed to keep them out of his food and water. Or you can do as we used to do with Mr. Murphy, our Poodle—we just secured his ears to the top of his head very gently with either hairpins or rubber bands.

# The Other Essentials

Here's a list of all the rest of the items you'll need:

**Puppy playpen**—This is a must, if you are to preserve your sanity. If you give a puppy the run of the house, he's going to strew his toys everywhere and piddle everywhere and, inevitably, will decide to gnaw on a leg of that 1880s table that Aunt Ethel willed you. Just as a playpen keeps a baby out of trouble, it will keep your puppy safe and removed from temptation. Don't run out and buy a $100 playpen because you're not going to need it for very long. Maybe you can pick one up at a garage sale or through an Internet auction site. Most puppies are content to spend time in a playpen through about their fourth month. If you take the pup out now and then, walk him, let him pee and play, he's going to be happy to curl up in his playpen with his toys and sleep most of the day. Change his toys from day to day to keep him amused. We had clients who bought one of those baby mobiles that you hang above a crib to amuse their puppy while he was in his playpen. It was a big hit. Don't forget to lay some newspapers on the floor of the playpen—despite your best efforts, the puppy's going to relieve himself there now and then.

**Baby gate**—Again, don't spend a fortune—a secondhand kiddie gate will do just fine. You'll pay three times as much for a gate at a pet store just because it says "dog" on it. Stamp PET on anything, and it costs twice as much, simply because the people who manufacture these things know that pet owners are pushovers. Find a safe area of your house where your puppy likes to spend time—maybe the kitchen, where the floor is easily mopped—and install the gates(s) to block off the room.

**Brush and comb**—A good all-around natural-bristle puppy brush and a steel comb (there are brushes and combs designed for smooth coats, curly coats, short coats, and long coats). Pet stores will try to sell you six kinds of hairbrushes in different sizes for different parts of the dog's body—a whisker brush, a topknot brush, a brush for the paws, all in puppy sizes, of course. This is nonsense. One brush is enough for now. Later, you'll get a brush designed for a grown dog.

**Doggie toothbrush**—If you start brushing your puppy's teeth every day right at the start, he will tolerate it and will need fewer expensive professional cleanings. A baby toothbrush will also do the job. In Chapter Nine, we tell you how to brush a dog's teeth. Regular toothbrushing will get the puppy used to having his mouth opened, should you need to peer inside to see what he's put into it, and it will make him less resistant to having the vet ask him to "open wide."

**Collar and leash**–Get your puppy used to the idea of wearing a collar from the day you bring him home. Collars are available in nylon or leather, and come either with flat buckles and holes to allow for adjustment or with quick release snaps in place of a buckle. These, too, are easily adjusted as the puppy grows. Some large pet stores now have do-it-yourself machines for making doggie name tags with the pup's name, address, and your phone number. Others have displays from which you can special-order the tag. When you buy a license for your dog, which is required in all states, you will get a metal registration-number tag that you should also attach to his collar.

From the age of about ten weeks, a puppy can be placed on-leash, a first step toward teaching him to heel.

**Housecleaning essentials**—You'll want to get one of those pet-hair pickup sticky rollers and a product such as Nature's Miracle, a liquid available at any pet store, which is great for mopping up accidents and neutralizing urine odor.

# Cages and Crates

Your puppy will need a dog crate, which is a cage by any other name. Here's the difference: A crate is made of molded plastic with a wire front; a cage is made of wire. Whichever you choose, expect to pay between $45 (for a smaller dog) and $200 (for a Giant breed). Size largely determines price. Crates come in sizes from extra small to extra large, in a rainbow of colors (another doggie fashion statement), and in top-loading and front-loading models. You will use the crate or cage to housebreak your puppy and, for his first few weeks at least, as his nighttime sleeping place.

Some of our clients use the molded plastic crates for housebreaking, feeling they are more like a den and make their puppies feel secure. We prefer a wire cage, as it allows the puppy to see all around and feel like he is part of the family. If you choose a wire cage, you can simply cover it with a large towel when you take the pup into your bedroom at night, which you should. You can buy a nylon crate pad, but an old towel or blanket will do nicely. If you use a blanket, make sure it's one with a tight weave. We had a client dog that snagged a nail on the thermal blanket in his crate, got all tangled up in the threads, and might have been strangled had the owner not discovered him in time. Need we tell you that old electric blankets aren't suitable for puppy crates?

Don't buy a puppy-sized crate or cage because your puppy's going to grow quickly and you'll soon be stuck buying a bigger crate. Buy the size that is appropriate for a full-grown dog of your breed and insert a wood or cardboard partition to block off the back, moving the partition back as the puppy grows. Or you can buy a crate or cage with a wire divider that snaps in and is adjustable. If your dog's not destined to be a world traveler, a wire crate seems to us a little more puppy-friendly.

One word of warning: There are puppies that are claustrophobic and will get quite hysterical when crated. They will bark incessantly, tremble and salivate excessively, and may actually bloody their noses or paws in an effort to get out. You should never force such a dog to stay in a crate. (Imagine a claustrophobic person being trapped in an elevator.) And these dogs definitely are not candidates for crate training, which we discuss in Chapter Four.

## Things Your Pup Really Doesn't Need

There are people making millions off pets. Think doggie galoshes, doggie raincoats, doggie designer collars. We had one little dog client that had his own trench coat and fedora. Now, there's no earthly reason for a dog—except maybe a very old dog or one living in a frigid climate—to have a coat or even a sweater. The dogs' own coats have natural oils that keep them warm. If you could ask those fancy dogs prancing down Rodeo Drive, the most chic street in chic Beverly Hills, on a sunny winter day they'd probably tell you that their little jackets with designer logos are damnably uncomfortable. As for doggie rain booties, they may be adorable (even if your dog doesn't think so) but, in fact, wearing them can soften the paw pads and make them vulnerable to injury. And we have yet to see a dog that enjoyed wearing a hat. Buttons and bows? All right, if you must, but make sure your dog can't swallow them. We've also seen dogs "marry" in wedding dresses and tuxes. Our view? People who do this to dogs have way too much time on their hands. Okay, we confess that we bought a rhinestone collar for Mr. Murphy, our Toy Poodle.

## Puppy's First Christmas

Do you melt just thinking about it? All those squeak toys, all those balls and chews, the tree . . .

Dog. Tree. Got the picture?

First, your puppy pees on the tree, gets himself all wrapped up in tinsel, and eats a few strands, then devours the chocolates Aunt Grace left. As the tinsel and chocolate are digesting, your puppy discovers the poinsettia, which looks good enough to eat—and will make him very sick.

For an encore, he topples the tree, sending it smashing into the fireplace. Merry Christmas.

If you want to keep your puppy safe, and keep your sanity, during the holidays, remember to:

- Place the tree in an area that can be gated to keep the puppy out.
- Unplug the Christmas lights at bedtime or when no one's at home.
- Place fragile ornaments high on the branches.
- Snuff out candles when leaving a room.
- Ask guests not to feed the puppy, and don't go wild yourself with yuletide puppy treats.
- Keep chocolates out of the dog's reach, and place poinsettia plants on high tables. Both are highly poisonous to dogs.

# The Homecoming

When you go to pick your puppy up from the breeder, you'll want to take a friend or family member along, as well as a lap towel, a roll of paper towels in case of an accident, and some plastic bags for disposing of used paper towels. If you're lucky, the puppy will have cooperated by taking care of business before leaving the breeder's house. Although as a rule dogs should be secured in their crates whenever riding in a car, we make an exception for homecoming day. It's unlikely that the pup has ever ridden in a car and he's going to be spooked by the strange sounds and vibrations. We think just this once it's a good idea to wrap him in a towel or blanket and have your passenger hold him securely in her lap, talking soothingly to the pup. You don't want one frightening experience to make the pup car-shy.

Within a day or two, it's a good idea to hold a family caucus to decide who's going to do what for the pup. Posting a schedule will remind children of their duties, which may include feeding the pup or taking him outside.

# The Family Doctor

No more than forty-eight hours after bringing your puppy home, you should take him to the vet—his family doctor—for his first checkup, and to schedule his immunizations, which should be completed by four months of age. Be sure to take with you his immunization record, which the breeder or the animal shelter will have given you. The vet will want to know the pup's birthdate, if you have it, and what, if any, deworming or heartworm medication he has taken. If the vet you have chosen does not have twenty-four-hour emergency care, you should locate an animal hospital near your home that does.

The best way to find a kind, competent vet is to ask for recommendations from friends. Before choosing a doctor you should make a get-acquainted appointment to determine whether this vet is right for you and your dog. Is the doctor personable? What about bedside manner? How experienced is he or she? We like a vet who will take the time to explain everything and will offer options rather than telling you, "This is what we have to do, yadda, yadda, yadda, and that'll be five hundred dollars."

# Just Say "Ahh . . ."

We also shy away from vets who come in, stick a thing down the dog's throat, stick another thing in the dog's ear, throw some pills at you, walk away, and say, "See me in two weeks." As the dog's owner, you have every right to know in detail what's going on. Beware, too, of overly aggressive vets. We've seen some who'll just pick the dog up by the collar, without so much as a hello, and take him howling out of the room. By observing the interaction between dog and vet, we actually let our dogs pick their doctors. Our dogs will run right up to some, but cower when others come near. If your pup hates going to the vet, it may be that it's just that vet that he hates.

There are lots of vets out there charging exorbitant prices, so you should comparison shop. In any event, we highly recommend getting health insurance for your pup. You'll find brochures at most vets' clinics. If you take out insurance while your dog's still a puppy, it is not prohibitively expensive. As with people, the older the dog, the steeper the premium.

# In Case of Emergency

You'll want to be prepared for natural and unnatural disasters. Because we live in southern California, where the earth periodically shakes, rattles, and rolls, we are keenly aware of the importance of having a pet emergency kit. An emergency kit should contain a two- to three-day supply of water and dry food in plastic containers, two bowls, the dog's collar and leash, a first-aid kit, and a blanket or towel. You should put in a copy of your pup's medical records, with a notation about any special medical or dietary needs, together with a photo of the dog. Store the kit in the garage or another place where you can find it quickly should you and your dog have to leave home with little or no warning. If there is a disaster, it's apt to be a confusing time for the dog, and you may not have time to put him on-leash. Familiar scents and landmarks could be destroyed, and he could easily become disoriented and get lost. That's when you'll be glad to have that photo to show around as you search.

## I'm Scared, Too

Who's going to be more jittery—you or your new puppy? It's a toss-up. But you've done your puppy-proofing, and the nursery is ready. Once home, the first thing the pup's going to want to do is to pee. Take him to the corner where you've laid down newspapers. He'll soon catch on that this is where he's supposed to go.

Then you should take your puppy directly to the area where he will spend most of his time for the next few months, the space that you've already gated. There the pup will find his toys, food, water bowls, and crate. Don't just bring your puppy home, plop him down, and head off to the white sales. Having just been separated from his mother and siblings, he needs to be with you and his new family, right in the center of the action. For the first fifteen minutes, it's a good idea to put him in his crate. A blanket tossed over the crate may make him feel more secure, and a hot-water bottle wrapped in a towel and placed in the crate may make him feel better about being in this strange place.

The pup should never be left in his crate all day while you're at work, but for short periods, puppies actually like being crated. It makes them feel secure, as though they had Mother's arms wrapped around them. Placing a T-shirt with your scent inside is also reassuring to the puppy. If your puppy is crated all day, he'll get into the habit of sleeping all day and keeping you up all night.

## Love Me and Leave Me Alone Awhile

A little cuddling is good, but don't allow family members to be picking the puppy up constantly. Let the puppy approach each family member when he is ready. It's fine for the children to pat the puppy and pick him up now and then—but not by the scruff of the neck. Always support a puppy's little bottom when handling him. The pup will want to be held continuously, but it's not good for him. His immune system isn't fully developed, so he's quick to pick up germs and is apt to get sick and throw up. Also, a puppy needs quiet time, which means no rock music, no TV blaring. And don't bring everybody you know over to see the new baby just yet.

## He's Family Now

The first important step with a new puppy is bonding. Training will come later. Your new puppy needs to feel that he belongs, and from the start he will have a strong desire to be part of this new family or pack. If at all possible, arrange for someone to be home with the puppy the first few days. One good plan is to arrange to pick the puppy up from the breeder on a Friday so you can be with him over the weekend. Remember, the pup's just been taken away from Mom and from his siblings.

Bonding means that you understand your puppy and he understands you. You will know when the two of you have bonded because he will listen to you and follow you, his pack leader, and look to you for guidance. A puppy that has bonded with you will trust you and that will make training him easier. There's nothing very complex about bonding. All you have to do is communicate to your puppy your love and affection and he will respond.

We talk baby talk to our dogs—and it works. The tone of your voice will convey to your puppy all he needs to know about how you feel about him. Dogs don't really understand words per se, but they do learn to react to combinations of sounds and to the tone of your voice. A blend of happy talk, patting, and hugging is a no-fail formula for bonding. We also sing to the dogs we take care of, and there's nothing funnier than seeing eight or nine dogs sitting in our kitchen, howling in unison as we sing. Dogs are very sensual creatures and they live by what they hear, smell, or see. They love contact. The more you love them, pat and kiss them, the more they will love you back.

# The Puppy Crazies

One day your puppy will suddenly jump up, run around, chase his tail, pounce on your sofa, bounce off your bed, toss his toys into the air and growl at them, and grab your shoes and dash with them from room to room as if running a puppy 500. We call this the puppy crazies. Your dog is not possessed. This is simply puppyspeak for "I want you to play with me."

You may want to growl back. We do a lot of puppy growling because that's what the pup's mommy does. It's a form of canine communication. There's our playful growl, and there's our enough-of-that growl. A puppy can tell the difference and knows that the enough-of-that growl means, "Ooh, I guess I shouldn't be doing this." We also smile at our dogs, and they smile back. That may sound weird, but it's true. Their little upper lips go up on the sides and we get a show of teeth. Puppies need to play, but you must teach your puppy to play on your terms. A puppy uses his mouth to play and may get too rough. You can stop this by holding the puppy firmly, but gently, by the loose skin under his ears, looking him directly in the eye, and saying, "No!" That means no biting, no rough stuff. And no playtime until he can behave.

Like kids, puppies love attention and will act up to get it. If the pup misbehaves, the best thing to do—within reason—is to ignore the transgression. Pretty soon the pup will figure out that his little scheme isn't working. Conversely, you'll want to lavish him with praise when he does something that pleases you.

## Sibling Rivalry

The puppy may be joining a household that has established pets. Fish don't count (although we once knew a dog aptly named Sushi that would have gobbled up every fish in her owner's prized aquarium, had she been able to reach them). Birds do count. The bird's well-being aside, bird droppings are very toxic to puppies. If there's a house cat, that cat's going to be the aggressor, so you must make sure the puppy doesn't get scratched. A safe way to make an introduction is to place one animal on one side of a baby gate, one on the other. In fact, this is a good time to introduce the dog to the cat, while the dog's at a size disadvantage; later, the dog won't be as apt to bully the cat. A cat that doesn't want to know about this four-footed intruder will just retreat up high until she figures out whether it's safe down below. Cats and dogs can live in perfect harmony if you raise them right and give them an equal amount of attention. But most puppies aren't really into cats at first, especially if the cat is the newcomer, and will give chase. If the cat stands her ground, the puppy's going to abandon the game because it's no fun.

Perhaps you have an older dog that came into your household as an adult and is pretty set in his ways. That dog may resent the frisky new arrival. One way to avert trouble is to let the older dog investigate the puppy while he is sleeping. Keeping a firm grasp on the older dog's collar, let him sniff around the pup. A little baby talk never hurt: "Here's a new baby. Kiss the baby. Good boy." Make sure the older dog has some quiet time alone with you for the first few weeks that the puppy's in the household. Older dogs usually wind up loving puppies to death, but you have to be careful because they'll want to paw the puppy and may get a little rough. If the older dog is pretty inactive, he's apt to be rather stoical. He'll just size up the situation and decide, "Look, I really don't want to be a puppy. You be a puppy and just leave me alone."

## Kids and Puppies: Red Alert

A puppy should never be left alone with a young child, no matter how sweet and docile the pup may be. Puppies scratch and nip. Small children don't comprehend that puppies don't enjoy having little fingers stuck in their eyes or having their tails tweaked, and they may respond by biting. A child can be shown the correct way to approach the puppy, with one hand held out, palm up, below the puppy's chin. No one should approach a puppy with a hand held above the dog's head, as the puppy's going to jump at it—a behavior you don't want to start. A puppy can jump up and knock down a small child and cause injury. Children scream when they get excited and this will frighten the puppy. If a child teases a puppy and then runs away, the puppy's going to give chase. Not a good idea—the pup may get the idea that chasing people is okay.

Some dogs are afraid of children simply because they have never been around them. If a child helps take care of the dog, filling his food bowl, going along on his walks, the puppy will come to understand that this little person is a member of his new pack.

We had a frantic call one morning from a client, a first-time dog owner with two children under six. It was very important to her that her children learn early on that responsibility comes with having a dog and she thought she'd been getting her message across. So, as you can

## Kids and Dogs

Children instinctively think of a puppy as a toy and may want to poke the puppy, ride him, or tweak his tail. Understandably, this may provoke an unfriendly response from the puppy.

- Children should never poke, hit, or pound on a puppy or stick their fingers in his mouth.
- Children should not touch or try to pat any puppy that growls, shows his teeth, or runs away with his tail between his legs.
- Children should never try to take toys, bones, or food away from a puppy.
- Children should not be allowed to startle a puppy that is sleeping.
- Children should never attempt to punish a puppy.
- If a puppy comes up to a child, the child should not run away, but stand still, avoiding eye contact. After a minute, the child should walk away quietly.

imagine, she was horrified to have to call and tell us that her children had fed the dog bubble gum. It took us two hours to extract pink goo from the whiskers of Weezer the Wirehaired Terrier. Children must be taught that puppies don't chew gum or eat candy.

# Puppy Pranks

Inadvertently, people will teach puppies to do things you really don't want them to do. Otis the Pug was only six weeks old when he came to live with his owner. Each morning as she dressed for work, she'd put Otis—all three pounds of him—on her bed so he could watch. When she had her back turned, he'd sneak into her makeup bag and steal brushes, lipsticks, and anything else he could chew on. So she began to play a little game with him, leaving the bag open and watching as he reached stealthily in with a paw. She found this irresistibly cute. Once he'd removed everything, she'd retrieve it all, saying, "Give me that, you little thief!" Otis also thought this was a great game. All was well until a friend came over one day and, before they adjourned to the living room to have coffee, the visitor put her handbag on the floor in another room. As they chatted, the pup's owner realized that Otis seemed suspiciously quiet. Upon investigation, she found that Otis had stolen a wallet, a lipstick, and a scarf from her friend's handbag and had squirreled his new treasures away in her bedroom. Mortified, she had to explain that she had a kleptomaniac canine.

You've heard of the mystery of the disappearing socks? Well, ours were vanishing, but not into the black hole of our clothes dryer. We discovered that one of our pups was stealing them from the bedroom, where we'd tossed them on the floor at day's end, and tucking them neatly into her doggie bed.

One of our Kritter Sitters spent hours picking out the just-right Christmas gift for her sister, a lovely piece of jewelry. When she arrived for her sister's holiday party, she found a roomful of people and a big pile of packages under the tree. Not wanting her tiny box to get lost, she slipped it onto a lower branch. The next day was Christmas and, eager to know how her sister liked her gift, she couldn't wait to call and ask. "What gift?" was the reply. No, she had not found a small box with gold and white wrapping. Three months passed, and both became convinced that the package had been swept up and thrown away in the clutter and confusion of Christmas morning. Then one day her sister called. She'd found the little box stashed neatly in a dark corner under her bed, together with other missing treasures deposited there by her Schnauzer, Sushi. The dog's stash included a silver pen, a bracelet, and $20 in bills.

# Bedtime!

When your pup stops bouncing around and just lies down with a far-away look in his eyes, it's bedtime. We've seen puppies nod off sitting upright, or even while eating. A tired puppy is a happy puppy, so you'll want to wear him out as bedtime nears. That means getting down on the floor on all fours and tossing a ball or a toy for him to retrieve. You may want to take him for a walk on-leash, but expect him to be a bit wobbly on those little legs at first. Establish a firm bedtime and stick to it. Your puppy's a creature of habit, and if you let him stay up until midnight now, you're going to have a dog that will keep you up until midnight for the rest of his life.

The first night in his new home can be really scary for your puppy. We suggest that you keep him secured in his crate in your bedroom. You may want to tuck in a hot-water bottle wrapped in that T-shirt with your scent. A nightlight may help keep the bogeyman away. If the crate is small, you might do as we do—hoist it up onto the bed while you're watching television until lights out. The puppy needs to know that he's not alone, and he will feel safe if he can see you.

Don't expect your puppy to sleep through the night until after three months, when his bladder gets a little bigger. Until then, he's pretty much like a baby and will need to piddle about every two hours. Dogs hate to piddle in their beds, so, if you lay newspapers on the floor, he'll head right for the papers when you let him out of his crate. And, yes, you will have to get up in the night to do that. (See Chapter Four.) The puppy will probably sound off to alert you that nature is calling.

# I'm Homesick

For the first few days, your puppy is going to miss his mother, even though he may be happy to be away from those pesky littermates that chewed his ears and were always rolling over on top of him. Some puppies will just want to cling to you for dear life, but you must be firm and establish a play-sleep-eat-pee routine from the start. If your puppy wakes up at night whining, it may not mean that he has to go. When a puppy is separated from his pack, he whines instinctively so that the others in the pack can find him. If you're pretty sure he doesn't need a bathroom break, don't pick him up. That will only encourage more whining. The better idea is to tap your hand on his crate and say, "No!" loudly and firmly. In time he will settle down.

If you notice him twitching in his sleep, don't be alarmed. It isn't some dreadful neurological disorder. Puppies do twitch as they snooze, and some will continue to do it into adulthood. It's okay—they're just dreaming. One night while we had several puppies in our care we heard a great commotion in the kitchen, a chorus of whimpering and howling. We tiptoed in and found three puppies sound asleep and howling at the top of their lungs, two puppies chasing rabbits in their sleep, with their little legs moving back and forth like crazy, and two others making loud sucking noises as they slept.

## Consistency Is the Key

During the day, half an hour of playtime followed by a mininap in his playpen is a good routine for the puppy. He may whimper to be picked up. He may howl. He may cry. It may hurt you worse than it hurts him, but you must not give in. If he's been exercised, if he's dry and safe and clean and fed, leave him alone. If you pick the puppy up every time he cries, he will cry just to get picked up. If you're lucky, you may get the perfect puppy, one that doesn't even whimper. If so, give your breeder a big kiss. You may want to place an old blanket in the playpen. Dogs like security blankets and will become fiercely attached to a certain blanket or towel and drag it everywhere.

Your puppy will quickly adapt to your schedule if you stick to it and will pretty much resist any change in his routine for the rest of his life. If you have been getting up at five in the morning, but switch to a job that allows you to sleep until eight, your pup's still going to want you up at five and will be quite annoyed if you don't oblige. As your puppy gets a little older, and you want to alter his schedule, you can—if you do it gradually. One way is to make his final pit stop later in the evening so you can get a little extra shut-eye in the morning. We have several clients who have given us the keys to their houses so we can come in early in the morning, take their dogs out, walk and feed them, and put them back in their sleeping areas—all while their owners snooze contentedly.

**4**

# Potty Training

**P**uppies don't wear training pants. Nor can you plop your puppy down on the toilet and persuade him to do "number one" or "number two."

Puppies pee and pee and pee. Your puppy will pee when he wakes up—just as a child pees in his diapers on waking. Your puppy will pee after he's been fed, pee after he's been played with. Whenever a puppy eats and drinks, something called the gastrocolic reflex kicks in. That, translated, means that within half an hour the puppy's going to have to eliminate. During those thirty minutes, you should be on house alert for telltale signs, such as crouching, pawing the ground, walking in circles, sniffing. When a puppy's got to go, he's got to go. We call this doing the duty dance.

Some puppies that are naturally shy pee at the sight of a human. Others pee when they're excited. Some just dribble when they become anxious or excited. If your puppy does any of these things, take heart—he will outgrow the behavior. There's no point in punishing him because dogs don't understand punishment after the fact. Your best defense is to restrict his playtime to a room that has neither carpet nor draperies.

Here's what to expect each day:

- Puppies 6 to 14 weeks old: 8 to 10 bathroom breaks
- Puppies 14 to 20 weeks old: 6 to 8 bathroom breaks
- Puppies 20 to 30 weeks old: 4 to 6 bathroom breaks
- Puppies 30 weeks to a year old: 3 to 4 bathroom breaks
  (This is where your patience finally gets rewarded.)

We saw a sweatshirt that pretty well summed up housebreaking: "Agenda for the Day—Let dog in, Let dog out, Let dog in, Let dog out, Let dog in."

# Crate Training

We are great believers in crate training, which works on the principle that the pup, being an instinctively clean animal, does not want to pee or poop where he sleeps, and he will be sleeping in his crate at least some of the time. To avoid making a mess, he will hold it in as long as possible (although those hapless pet store puppies may have become quite used to the idea of sleeping in their own messes). If you've bought a crate large enough for an adult dog, which is what we recommend, you can simply partition it off, moving the divider back as the pup grows. At all times, the crate should be just large enough to allow the puppy to stand comfortably, turn around, and lie down. Otherwise, he may just go to the rear of the crate and take care of matters.

Some dog owners resist the idea of crating, seeing the crate as some kind of doggie prison. But the truth is that most pups actually feel more secure in a crate. A dog is, after all, a den animal.

# Thinking Ahead

Before bringing your puppy home, you must decide whether you are going to paper-train or crate-train him. The place you've chosen should be made ready, because the first thing he's going to want to do once home is to let go. Whether you're going to crate-train or paper-train him, it's important that you not keep moving his toilet. Dogs are creatures of habit, and the pup will just become confused and make mistakes.

When you crate-train, you put the puppy in his crate with his security towel, place a treat or a favorite toy inside, and latch the door. Don't push or shove him in, just gently place one paw, then the other, inside. His curiosity—and the inducement of that toy or treat—will get the better of him. If you have a wire crate, you should first remove his collar, which could snag on the wire. He will fuss and carry on at first. You must ignore him. Covering a wire crate with a towel will help to make it feel more denlike and the puppy feel more secure. After twenty minutes or so, take the puppy out of his crate and to a designated area outdoors and wait for him to perform. If he does, kiss him, praise him, and bring him back inside to play for half an hour in a secured area, such as a playpen. Then it's back to his crate. This is his special place.

Gradually, you should increase the time in-crate to two hours at a stretch. Do not take the puppy out if he cries, unless the protests go on for so long that you think there might be unfinished business. That's unlikely. Puppies figure out pretty quickly that they'd better get it all done when they have the chance so they won't have to sit in a mess. Should the puppy make a mistake in his crate, don't scold him. Maybe he was left too long. If so, cut back on his in-crate time for a few days. You'll soon get to know his limitations. Rarely will puppies mess in their crates. The pup that does this may be exhibiting anxiety, possibly as a result of having been taken too soon from his mother, and may need the help of a dog behaviorist.

## The Daily Routine

You must make a schedule and stick to it. The puppy's schedule can be adapted to fit yours, but here are some general guidelines:

> 7-7:30 A.M. WAKE-UP TIME: Take the puppy from his crate and di-rectly outside, always to the same spot. Bring him in, feed him breakfast, and, twenty minutes later, take him back outside. After about ten minutes' playtime, return him to his crate to nap.

MIDMORNING: Take the puppy from his crate and directly outside. More playtime, followed by in-crate nap time.

NOON: Take the puppy outside, bring him in for lunch, then take him outside twenty minutes later. Place him in his crate to nap.

MIDAFTERNOON: Take the puppy outside. Follow with playtime, then crate rest.

5-6 P.M.: Take the puppy outside, bring him in for dinner, and take him outside twenty minutes later. Follow with playtime.

7-8 P.M.: Take the puppy outside, follow with ten minutes' playtime before putting him in his crate to rest.

11 P.M.: Bedtime: Take the puppy outside, then bring him into your bedroom in his crate to sleep.

3 A.M.: Take the puppy outside. (Sorry)

## Mistakes Will Happen

Your puppy should be supervised at all times while he is out of his crate or he will make mistakes. Most puppies will learn the ropes in four to six weeks. That may seem like an eternity if you're cleaning up the accidents, but the puppy really would rather go outside and he will learn. Remember the old joke about never having seen anyone go off to college wearing diapers? Well, very rarely is there a dog that cannot be housebroken by the age of three months. If the puppy pees continuously, or if he has diarrhea, this is most likely a medical problem—a urinary tract infection or intestinal parasites—and should be checked out by your vet. Dietary changes can also cause diarrhea.

Even with the most cooperative of puppies, housebreaking is a real challenge. The key is consistency. You must keep track of each time you take the puppy outside. (If you've been keeping a "baby book"— we hope you have—write it down in there.) You will learn your puppy's particular bowel and bladder habits by trial and error, but the rule of thumb is to take the puppy outside on-leash twenty minutes after each meal. He will take short naps in his crate throughout the day and, as soon as he wakes, you should take him outside. You will also need to do this several times during the night for the first few weeks. It takes a while for his little bladder to develop fully. The puppy will cry to let you know when he's got to go.

# The Catchphrase

Each time you take the puppy from his crate and head for the door, repeat a catchphrase, such as "Want to go pee-pee?" Use the same door each time and don't carry him there—let him walk so he'll learn the routine. At about five months, he will make the connection and when you say, "Want to go pee-pee?" he will head for the door. Outside, lead him to a spot you will have designated and give him about ten minutes to perform. When he does, lavish him with praise, carrying on as though he had just done something brilliant such as discover the canine equivalent of the theory of relativity. You might want to use another catchphrase, such as "Way to go!" Always take him to the same spot so the odor will help remind him why he's there. After months of hearing "Way to go!" the puppy will begin to associate it with his bathroom function and the words alone will likely trigger the urge. (This can come in very handy later when you're taking car trips with your dog and want to coordinate his bathroom breaks with yours.)

If you have a bird in the house, beware of where you utter your catchphrases. We once had a cockatiel that picked up on ours. At three in the morning we'd be lying in our beds and we'd hear this damned cockatiel croaking, "Want to go pee-pee?" Well, of course all our puppies would come running. We found someone who really wanted that cockatiel.

# But It's Saturday . . .

You still have a life. That means your puppy is going to have to adapt to it—within reason. Unfortunately, he can't distinguish between night and day, weekdays and weekends. Taking away his water about three hours before bedtime probably will gain you a few hours' sleep. If you're a night person, you can feed your puppy his dinner later and his bathroom schedule will adjust itself accordingly. At night, move his crate into your bedroom under your watchful eye. If this is a hassle— say you live in a two-story house—you'll be wise to invest in a second crate. By six months of age, the puppy should stop having to wee-wee in the middle of the night and you can get a good night's sleep. If he hasn't stopped, it may be because he is lonely. If you've moved his crate out of your bedroom, you may have to move it back in for a while.

You can't expect a puppy under six months of age to hold it all in for more than four or five hours. If you must leave your puppy alone that long, he will need food and water and, well, you know what follows. If you don't want him peeing and pooping all over your house, a crate is the solution. If no one can be at home from nine to five, we recommend strongly that for the first six months you have a friend, a neighbor, or a dog walker come in at midday to feed the puppy and take him outside.

# Dog In, Dog Out . . .

Keeping in mind the twenty- to thirty-minute rule, you will want to keep a strict schedule for taking the puppy outside. He must understand that when he's put on-leash and led out the door, this is serious business, not fun and games. No lollygagging, no stopping to mark every petunia. Puppies can seem to take forever, sniffing around and carrying on. After all, everything is new to them—the bugs, the flowers, and the grass. The first few times, he may think this is playtime. Lead him to his spot and give him ten minutes to get on with the business at hand. "Good dog!" is the proper response after he performs. If you praise the puppy extravagantly for going outside, and use only the gentlest of admonitions when he makes a mistake in the house, he will learn quickly that it's better to go outside. You want to be certain that he's finished before taking him back inside. Once inside, he must be either in his crate or under your watchful eye.

Rewarding him with a treat every time he performs promptly isn't a good idea. A smart pup will figure out pretty quickly that if he produces a thimbleful of urine on command he'll be rewarded. So what happens? You take him back inside and he lets go like Niagara Falls. An occasional treat's okay and may keep the pup motivated. A nice walk after he's done his toileting is the best treat. If the puppy does not perform within ten minutes, return him to his crate and try again in about an hour.

# You're Getting There

Very gradually, you will want to increase the length of time the puppy spends in his crate before being taken outside. In time, you will be able to leave the crate door open overnight or for short periods during the day and have no mistakes. But a puppy that is being crate-trained should not have the run of the house unless he has just been taken outside. You don't want him to start making mistakes—"Hey, this beats putting on that leash and going out in the dark."

A dog that's being crate-trained should be exercised vigorously before being crated for the night, or for any long period. If he's had all his shots, he may enjoy romping with the neighbor pooches. Or you may want to play fetch-the-ball or take him to the park or for a brisk walk.

Never use the crate to punish or discipline your puppy. The crate's purpose is to teach the puppy to hold it in, so you don't want to confuse the two issues. After about a week, you should be able to leave the door of the crate open overnight, and from time to time during the day, and find no puddles on your floor.

# Paper Training

Paper training may be convenient for you, but we think it is a poor solution except for dog owners who live in high-rise apartments, are in ill health, or for other reasons are unwilling, or unable, to take their pups outside. It also is an option for those who cannot be at home during the day to crate and uncrate the puppy.

Paper training won't really housebreak your puppy. Anytime he feels the urge, he's apt to just head for the papers instead of asking to be taken outside. Or he may just let go in the same general area where the papers are. That's because he has not been taught that the house is not his toilet.

But if you must paper-train, here's how: You'll need to store up a good supply of newspapers because it's going to take two to three weeks to housebreak your pup. First, block off a room with those baby gates, preferably the kitchen, bathroom, laundry room, or another noncarpeted area where the puppy can have free run. Just as you place the crate-trained pup in his crate before leaving the house for a long period, you confine the paper-trained pup to this area. Cover the floor with a large plastic sheet and then with several layers of newspaper. Don't close the door—the puppy will likely become anxious, lonely, and stressed out. When you remove the soiled papers each day, leave a damp sheet on top with the pup's urine odor. This will attract him back to the same spot. By the sniff test he'll figure it out—"Oh, that's where I pee."

In three to seven days, your puppy will have established a pattern of going to the same spot. This is when you remove the rest of the newspapers, leaving only about an inch-thick stack of fully opened papers. With any luck, you'll be able to catch him in the act, distract him by clapping your hands, scoop him up and take him, and his newspapers, to a spot outdoors. When you place the papers on the grass, he'll probably get the idea right off. The transition from indoors to outdoors should take about a month, after which you no longer need to worry about newspapers. But you will very likely have to worry about accidents in the house.

Some dogs aren't candidates for paper training. We had a client dog, Rover, that took one look at the newspapers his owner had laid down for him and decided, "Oh, boy, another toy!" In no time he became the shredmaster of the Western world.

## Tether Training

Some people who have the luxury of being home all day with their puppies report success with tether training. Here's how it works: You attach a three-to-four-foot leash to the pup's collar and either tether the leash to your belt, so the puppy is never out of your sight as you go about your chores, or else tether it to a piece of furniture in a designated room. If the pup's tied to you, his body language will let you know when he has to go outside. If he's tied to a piece of furniture, the idea is that the leash must be too short to let him maneuver away from any mess he might make, the same principle as in crate training. We think a crate is better. A dog that's crated can't chew up your baseboards. Never tether a dog while you are out of the house, as he could become entangled in his leash and injure himself. When tethering your puppy, give him a chewy toy to distract him. Make note of the time elapsed since the pup was taken outside. If he begins to whine, it may be walk time. If it's not yet time, ignore the whining.

## Spare the Rod: Mop Up, Move On

People yell at their dogs because they think that gives them the upper hand. They're wrong. The dog-owner relationship is based on mutual trust, not on intimidation. Besides, dogs don't register guilt. When you yell at your puppy for peeing on your carpet, you're not teaching him that what he just did was wrong. He can't understand that. The only thing he'll understand is that being caught is wrong.

So you've just cleaned the house and are relaxing in front of the TV and you look over to see that Rover's taken a dump on your white rug. Don't panic. Just reach for the paper towels and the Nature's Miracle or another great liquid product, Outright, both of which will get rid of the odor. Both are widely available in pet stores or through catalogs. Nature's Miracle makes a dandy little device, a black-light unit that you plug into any outlet. When you shine the light on your carpet, it shows just where your pup has peed. What you can see, you can spray, which will keep the carpet odor-free. This is important, as a dog is likely to return to an area where he has left an odor and do it again. And just think what a good giggle your puppy will have, watching you crawling around on the rug waving that little lamp.

We don't believe in rubbing a puppy's nose in his mistake. This is both futile and disgusting. You'll risk winding up with a dog that is head-shy, a dog that cowers and turns away and gets really weird when you reach down to pet him. Dogs don't make mistakes to test your patience. Usually, they make mistakes because you have neglected to take them outside on schedule. A firm "No!" will suffice if you catch the puppy in the act. After the fact, forget it. He won't associate any kind of reprimand with something that he did even minutes before. If you're lucky enough to catch the puppy in the act, pick him up and head for the door, repeating your catchphrase. One caveat: Don't interrupt the puppy midpoop or midpee because he may become afraid to do his business, even outdoors—"Maybe I'll just hold it until I pop because the last time I tried to go, she was throwing a tizzy." Obviously, this could lead to medical problems.

## Don't Tempt Fate

Once your puppy is housebroken, you don't want to set him up for failure by giving him the run of the house while you're gone. You're apt to return home to find a little gift in the middle of your white brocade sofa. If there are going to be mistakes, let them be in spots where it is easy to mop up. Before going to work, secure the puppy in the kitchen, behind a baby gate, or in the bathroom or the garage. Don't forget to leave water and toys for him.

It's during the housebreaking stage that lots of people give up and give their dogs away. They're tired. They go to the movies and come back four hours later only to find that the dog has relieved himself on their down comforter. If this happens, you must ask yourself, "Did he do this because he was mad that I left him alone, or did he really have to go to the bathroom?" Some dogs will do it just to get even. There's nothing you can do about that except to confine them when they are alone.

You may want to keep your furniture covered until your pup is housebroken. Just take some big towels that you can plop in the washing machine and wrap them around the ends of your chairs and sofas. For some reason we can't explain, dogs only pee on the ends of things—the end of the bed, the end of the couch, the corner of a chair. If you don't want your living room to look as though Miss Havisham lives there, you might try the aluminum foil maneuver instead. A sheet of aluminum foil placed on a chair or sofa makes an awful racket when the puppy jumps up. One jump is usually enough. We had a client who covered her sofa in bubble wrap. When her puppy jumped up, his little nails dug in, popping the bubbles and scaring him to death. It worked.

## Piddle Pads

There are a few dog owners who just don't want to know about housebreaking. Perhaps because they live in a high-rise apartment, or because they can't or don't want to be bothered to walk their dogs, they opt for piddle pads. These are plastic-lined absorbent mats, available under several brand names at pet stores, that are a pup's permanent indoor toilet. Teaching a puppy to use one of these pads is very similar to training him to newspaper. But there's one big difference. The dog that's taught to use a piddle pad is not even partially housebroken. He has no concept of going outside and, should his owner forget to put down a pad, will relieve himself wherever he chooses. We don't really approve of these pads. For one thing, they smell awful, even if changed regularly. For another, we think it's terrible to keep a dog cooped up inside all the time with no chance to explore and to interact with other dogs and with people. However, we make an exception in the case of a semi-invalid or a frail elderly person who otherwise would not be able to keep a loving pet. Better than piddle pads, in our view, is a sod box. These are not available commercially, but can easily be made of redwood. The box should be about three feet by three feet. First, line it with plastic and then with sod from a nursery. The grass will last longer if watered daily, but it should be changed every week, as it gets awfully pungent. The solid litter must be scooped out daily.

**5**

# Bringing Up Baby:
# 1 to 4 Months

**J**ust as surely as a newborn baby coming home from the hospital disrupts the entire household until a routine is established, a new puppy will move in and take over.

Ideally, your puppy will be twelve weeks old when he comes to you. Puppies separated too soon from the litter tend to become overdependent, timid around other dogs, suffer great separation anxiety, and be fearful of—and possibly aggressive toward—strangers.

By twelve weeks, your puppy will have totally developed hearing and vision, pretty good motor skills, and a decent attention span, and will have learned from his mother and his litter that certain behaviors, such as growling and biting, are not socially acceptable.

Now it's up to you to raise a well-behaved dog. He doesn't speak your language, nor you his, so early on you must find a way to communicate with him. "No" and "Good dog" are words he'll get the gist of pretty quickly. A sharp "No!" each time he jumps on someone or bites or scratches someone should get your message across. Of course, it's just as important that you praise him when he stops doing these things.

## Here, Regis! Regis??

So you've named your pup Regis and he just stares blankly at you when you call, "Here, Regis!" That's only normal. It may take him several

---

### ⟨⟩ DID YOU KNOW? ⟨⟩

Did you know that puppies' eyes and ear canals open when they are between ten and fourteen days old—but the pups have limited eyesight and hearing until they are about six weeks old?

## Please Don't Call Me Beauregard

We won't go so far as to say that you can damage a puppy psychologically by what you name him. We once had a perfectly well-adjusted client dog named Freeway because that's where she was found. The probable truth is that dogs don't recognize their names, only the general inflection in your voice. A pup named Ashley (currently a very popular moniker) will probably perk up her ears when you say Kelly or Chelsea or another word ending in a similar sound.

Forget Fido. "People" names for dogs are very much in vogue. We've had dogs named Linda, Amanda, Dustin, Jerry-Lee, Julie, Lucy, Marilyn, Sophie, Oliver, Daisy, Nicholas, and Sammy.

Among our favorite moniker matches: Bentley the Maltese, Thurston the Chocolate Lab, Dachshunds Bogey and Bacall, Marble the mutt, Sparkle the Wheaten Terrier, Pugs Chrissie and Gabby, Pretzel the Whippet, Gracie the Golden Retriever, Winston the Fox Terrier, and Bizet the Jack Russell.

Not long ago the ASPCA polled dozens of veterinarians and came up with 300,000 pet names, from which they culled the top 30 in popularity. Max and Sam topped the list, but there were also old standbys like Lucky and Buddy. Other winners: Lady, Brandy, Baby, Pepper, Jake, Bandit, Tiger, Samantha, Charlie, Sheba, Patches, Tigger, Rusty, and Buster.

weeks to recognize that the new sound you're always making is his name. What you want to avoid is using his name in a negative fashion, as in "Naughty Regis!" He'll be sure he's going to be punished every time you call him and will take off in the opposite direction. Your puppy will make mistakes at first, but you must not yell at him. He will already be nervous, and yelling will only make him fearful. When that happens, you're off on the wrong foot and paw. Be as gentle as possible while you let him explore his new surroundings, sniff around his new home, and get to know his new family members. You want to be his teacher, not his disciplinarian. First impressions are the most important and your new puppy will remember everything you do now, and especially the tone of your voice. Just as infants walk and talk at different times, puppies develop on their own timetables.

People ask us when they should start training their puppies. If by training they mean obedience school, the answer is around six months. However, training starts at home—and it should start the day you bring the puppy home. By that, we mean teaching him simple commands through which he'll learn what's acceptable and what's not. (In Chapter Eight, we discuss behavior problems and solutions.) Many places, such as park and recreation departments, offer puppy preschools and, once your pup's completed his shots—around four or five months—he will enjoy socializing with other dogs his own age. And you'll have the fun of showing him off.

You will be taking your puppy in your car, if only to the vet, and will need some kind of car restraint. Whatever you do, don't let an immature dog loose in the car. He's apt to wind up in your lap—hardly conducive to safe driving. Or, worse yet, he could get all tangled up in the brake or accelerator pedal. You can buy a harness or a seat belt to restrain your puppy. Safest of all, we think, is a securely anchored crate that you keep permanently in your car. If buying a car, you may want to consider a station wagon or an SUV. Some of our more well-heeled clients actually buy cars to accommodate their puppies.

## An Ounce of Prevention

Puppies get from their mothers' milk a passive immunity that sees them safely through the first few weeks of life. Then it's necessary to have them vaccinated to build up their own immune systems. By the time you bring your puppy home at twelve weeks, he should have had a series of shots to protect him against distemper and measles. The breeder will give you his immunization record.

Between fourteen and sixteen weeks, the pup should be inoculated against DHLPP (distemper, hepatitis, leptospirosis, parainfluenza, and parvovirus) and rabies. If you live in a region where Lyme disease is a threat, your vet may recommend immunizing the puppy. Don't let your puppy go outside, or near other dogs, until the above series of shots is completed. If you're certain that another dog is up to snuff on his shots, and in good health, your pup may play with him.

Then there are worms. The truth is that most puppies have worms, as they become infected from larvae dormant in the mother dog. A good breeder will have had the pup wormed twice before the age of six weeks. Now it's up to you to see that he is tested regularly. Your vet will remind you. If worms are not done away with, they can stunt the puppy's growth, and reinfection is common. Your vet may also recommend vaccination against heartworm, a parasite that is prevalent in warm climates.

## What's My Puppy Saying?

As you cannot ask your puppy what he's doing—well, you can, but he's not going to tell you—it's important that you understand doggie body language.

Your puppy may crouch, raising one paw and leaning to one side. Or he may suddenly leap backward and take off like a bullet, hoping you'll give chase. Or he may splay his front legs and stand with his head down and his bottom up. All of these behaviors probably mean "I want to play."

Until three months of age, puppies should be considered infants. Like all infants, they require loving attention—and plenty of it. They are just starting to develop their little personalities. During this time, socialization is vital. The puppy that's just sort of left to fend for himself, isolated from his family for long periods, is going to develop undesirable behaviors such as chewing and barking.

Sometimes your pup will puzzle or disappoint you. Puppies are sweet, loving—and unpredictable. You may expect him to all but turn cartwheels because you have just showered him with words of praise. If instead he just sort of goes "Eh . . . ," it's not that he doesn't want to be praised. He simply needs hands-on praise until he understands all those nice words. Your puppy may drop off to sleep while you're playing with him. It's not that you bore him. And he doesn't have narcolepsy. It's just that he's sleepy. Remember—he's a baby. We've seen puppies nod off while eating their dinner.

To help a child and a puppy establish a good relationship, you might want to enlist your child to help teach the puppy to maneuver stairs. At about three months, the puppy should no longer need to be carried up and down. If you have a very small dog and very steep stairs, it may take longer. Place the puppy on the first step and have the child kneel at the foot of the stairs and just gently nudge him forward. He'll catch on.

## Separation Anxiety

Separation anxiety is a serious problem. Dogs that are left alone for long periods of time may chew doors, rip down curtains, try to jump through plate glass, chew themselves, and destroy furniture. A lot of these dogs, sadly, wind up in animal shelters.

When you have to leave your puppy, you don't want to make a big deal out of it. None of this "Oh, honey, Mommy loves you so much. Now, be a good baby and don't be sad." Do that and the dog will be wondering if he'll ever see you again. Some dogs just think you're leaving forever and you can't tell a dog, "It's okay. I'm just running down to the supermarket."

If your puppy reacts strongly when you leave the house and you think separation anxiety is going to be a problem, here's what to do: Go out the door, stay outside a couple of minutes, come back in, give the dog a doggie cookie, go back out for twenty minutes, come back in, go back out and stay out for an hour. By then, the dog will know he is not going to be abandoned. He doesn't know when you're coming back, but if you've done everything right, he really doesn't care. If the dog keeps barking each time you leave, you come back in and say firmly but calmly, "No barking. No, no, no." Don't yell at the dog.

A few puppies are so high-strung that their separation anxiety can only be eased with tranquilizers, but most will relax once they get the idea that good-bye isn't forever. Dogs that live with other dogs tend to be far less anxious. They'll sit with each other, talk to each other, probably bitch about you—"So she's gone again, eh?" Of course, two can think up more mischief than one. We once left two playful puppies in our kitchen with a brand-new doggie bed. We came home to a blizzard of polyfoam snowflakes—and two of the happiest dogs you'd ever want to see.

Puppies seem to find toilet-paper rolls fascinating and, if bored, will unwind the entire roll and drape the paper around the house. If your puppy starts doing this, place about a dozen pennies in an empty soda can, tape it shut, and prop it on top of the toilet-paper holder. When the puppy pulls on the roll, the can will fall with a great clanging of coins that is guaranteed to send the puppy running and to break him of the habit.

At our house, we leave the television on twenty-four hours a day for the benefit of our canine boarders. For one thing, it filters out noises from outside that could potentially set off a chorus of barking. It's also company. A dog will actually watch TV, especially if there's another animal on the screen. You can buy tapes of dogs for dogs, and they're fascinated by them, just as babies are fascinated by other babies. We had a Golden Retriever, Clancy, that was a real Dudley Moore fan and couldn't be pried away from *Milo and Otis*. Other dogs will sit, transfixed, watching *Babe, Beethoven, 101 Dalmatians,* or *Turner and Hooch.*

Some of our clients dash home from their offices at noon just to take their dogs for a walk. Others hire a pet sitter or dog walker. The first day that you must leave the puppy, it's a good idea to have a friend or neighbor come in and play with him. Puppies aren't ready to be left alone all day until they're about six months old.

## Don't Fence Me In

Puppies are not meant to be isolated. We knew of a Doberman that basically was raised in a bathroom. For six months, that poor dog was locked in that bathroom every day, cut off from everyone and everything, until the couple came home from work. What happened was that the dog became nontrusting and introverted. Other people will just stick their puppy outside, which is a sure way to alienate both the dog and your neighbors. The puppy will bark nonstop and try to dig his way to freedom.

A dog that's given something appealing to distract him—a bone or a dog biscuit—when you must leave him alone is apt to forget, at least for a while, that he's suffering separation anxiety. A Kong toy filled with peanut butter will take the pup hours of licking and chewing, fighting and biting, to get all the peanut butter—and by that time you're home. Or you can put a couple of jerky treats inside a chew toy, making one easy to reach, the other almost impossible to get to. There are also little plastic cubes that you fill with dry food. The pup will push one of these around the floor for four hours, expending all his energy trying to figure out why food falls out of the tiny holes sometimes but other times just won't. He'll be so busy he won't remember how long you've been gone. Dogs don't know a minute from an hour.

# Ouch! It's a Tooth

At about four months, your puppy's baby teeth will fall out. This will probably happen without any assistance from you. Nonetheless, when you brush your puppy's teeth—as you should every day—it's a good idea to watch for any baby teeth that don't want to depart to give the permanent teeth room to come in. This becomes a matter for a vet.

Teething is very annoying to a puppy, just as it is to a baby. His gums itch and get sore, and the pup's response is to chew. And chew. And chew. He will chew everything in sight, from lamp cords to shoes. We had a client who called us in shock. Her Bulldog had eaten four pairs of her Ferragamos—$1,200 worth of shoes! Naturally, the dog didn't go for her Keds. The same client left a new $1,300 Italian suit on his bed—with the bedroom door open—only to return home to find that Goldie, his Great Dane, had feasted on the cuffs. That story did have a happy ending. Because the suit had been purchased on an American Express card, the card owner filed a claim, sending American Express the suit together with a picture of the dog that ate the suit. He got a refund.

Dogs can't open closed doors. We have yet to see a dog grab a knob with his paw and twist. But they will open doors left ajar, and they will open swinging doors. Just by watching you, they'll figure out how to do this in a hurry.

Rule one for dealing with a teething puppy: Do not leave anything you value that is chewable at puppy height. What they can't reach, they can't chew. Rule two: Redirect the puppy's attention to something he's allowed to chew. We recommend buying a few good rubber toys and chilling them in the freezer so they soothe the puppy's gums as he chews. Puppies also love chewing on ice cubes, or chicken or beef bouillon cubes that have been frozen in ice trays. Strips of wet cloth, tied in knots and frozen, also feel good on the puppy's angry gums as he chews.

# Flee! Flea

Unless you live above a thousand feet in altitude, your puppy is going to have fleas. Fleas are equal opportunity pests, proliferating in every state.

But fleas have finally met their match in a little pill called Program, which can safely be given to puppies starting at the age of three months. You just give it to your puppy once a month, disguising it inside a piece of cheese or something else he likes. Other products, such as Advantage, which you squirt on the scruff of the puppy's neck, work in the same way—they actually interfere with the flea's life cycle. Until recently, all of these products were available only through veterinarians, and were quite pricey, but are now widely available through mail-order catalogs.

Despite your best efforts, it's almost impossible to have a flea-free house. Fleas live in your yard and you track them in. Once inside, they make a beeline for your puppy, then take up residence in your carpet, draperies, or bedding. So you must be aggressive in fighting fleas, especially in hot weather. Should you feel something nipping at your ankles, it's time to shampoo the puppy, shampoo your rugs, and call in a company such as Fleabusters that will deflea the carpets—without smothering your house in some awful toxic chemical so dangerous that every living thing must first be removed.

If your puppy has had all of his shots (at three to four months), it's safe to take him to a professional groomer for a bath and flea dip. If he's too young, bathe him yourself. Pet stores and pet supply catalogs have flea-killing shampoos that are safe for puppies this age.

There are those who will tell you that a flea collar permeated with insecticide will take care of any flea problems. Who are they kidding? A flea collar will kill fleas, all right, every one of them that happens to be hiding in that one-inch band under the collar. A flea collar is not going to kill those on the tip of the tail or the bottoms of the feet. That's why there are flea shampoos and flea dips. Don't waste your money. In any event, a puppy under the age of two months should never wear a flea collar.

There are topical flea sprays and powders available at the super-market. Don't buy them. They're dangerous. We've seen dogs develop severe skin problems from these products. Others have quit eating. One dog we knew lost all her hair—and it never grew back. If you're going to use a topical product, make it Zodiac or another of the brands avail-able only through a vet or from catalogs. Puppies under two months of age should not be powdered or sprayed.

If you opt for Program or Advantage, fleas should not be a real prob-lem. The little devils that get tracked in from outside can be controlled by frequent vacuuming of furniture and carpets. Your puppy's bedding should be washed as frequently as you wash your own, and dried on the high-heat cycle to kill any flea eggs.

## Baby's Bathtime

Fleas or no fleas, when your puppy is around three to four months of age, he is ready for his first bath. If his shots are completed, you may want a professional groomer to do the job. Or you may opt to wash your puppy at home, which will save you money. You'll know when he needs a bath. Puppies do get pungent. Unless he's had a run-in with a skunk, or a roll in the mud, your puppy shouldn't be bathed more than once a week.

Here's how to get started:

- ✔ Brush and comb your puppy to get rid of mats and knots. Bathing won't remove these and will only cause them to tighten up, and your puppy's coat will be history.
- ✔ Place cotton in the puppy's ears to prevent water from getting in.

✔ A puppy—unless he's one of the really big breeds—can just be popped into the kitchen sink and bathed with a nozzle spray. For the big guys, a hose in the backyard is a better idea.

✔ To protect the puppy's eyes, never pour shampoo on his head. Pour it into your hands, make a lather, and with this gently and carefully wash his face.

✔ After shampooing and thoroughly rinsing, roll the puppy up in a thick towel and hand-dry him.

✔ Place your blow dryer on a special stand, widely available where pet supplies or beauty supplies are sold, to keep your hands free. Starting at the pup's head, keep brushing his coat while using the dryer on a warm, not hot, setting. All dogs, except wash-and-wear dogs, should be blow-dried, as it makes their coats fuller and stimulates their skin, bringing out the natural oils.

Dog skin is far more sensitive than human skin and given to dryness. That's because it's only one layer thick, while yours has three layers. That fancy shampoo that you bought on your last visit to Salon Bon Ton is fine for you, but not for your puppy. It's formulated to remove oils. Puppy needs a shampoo that removes dirt without removing oils. Neutrogena is great for dogs with sensitive skin. Don't decide. "Oh, I'll just use some of this dishwashing detergent." That will strip all the oils from the puppy's fur. Think about it: "Cuts grease!" There are whitening shampoos for dogs with light-colored coats, shampoos for dark-coated dogs, and shampoos for itchy dogs. Your vet can advise you as to which is best for your puppy. Many of the products used by professional groomers are not sold at retail, but pet supply catalogs offer a full range of shampoos and conditioners. Steer away from soaps with perfumes, which are irritants and can trigger allergies. Hot-oil products designed for your hair are wonderful for dogs' skin, and crème rinses will tame their fur. Be sure to rinse and rinse, as soap that is left on can dry the skin.

Puppies do get dandruff. It's quite common, and in dogs with dark fur those little white flakes are very visible. Basically, the problem is dry skin, called dander. A puppy's lubricating glands don't mature until he's about four months old. It's nothing to worry about, although the dandruff may cause itching. We like to use oatmeal shampoo on our puppies, as it's very calming to the skin.

## Doggie Hairdressers

If you have a high-end dog—either one that is longhaired or a breed like a Poodle that you think should have the proper coiffure—you're probably going to want to establish an ongoing relationship with a professional groomer. In southern California, designer doggie salons abound. For various reasons, certain other breeds of dog should also be groomed professionally. Some long-eared dogs, for example, need to have their ears cleaned in a certain way.

Another good reason to use a groomer is to have the dog's nails trimmed properly. If you don't know what you're doing, you can easily cut the quick. Big dogs sort of file their nails as they walk on cement. But if you let a small dog's nails grow too long, the dog will walk on his nails, which can force them up into the pads and cause infections. A puppy should have regular nail trimmings—every six to eight weeks—starting at the age of three months. Long nails can be hazardous. A pup can get a nail snagged in clothing or on a car seat and have it ripped right out. We think trimming is best done at a grooming salon, but if you are very careful, you can do it at home.

Here's how:

- Buy a pair of special clippers available at pet stores. These have a hole into which you insert the pup's nail to prevent you from cutting into the quick, the pink part of the nail containing nerves and blood vessels. On dark-nailed dogs, this can be hard to see. Better to cut too little than too much.

- The puppy is apt to be afraid of the clippers, and anxious about what you're doing. You may want to take it easy, trimming one nail a day. Handling the pup's feet for a few days beforehand, and for a few minutes before starting the trimming, will help him get used to the idea.
- Cut just at the point where the nail curves downward, no higher. Think of it as trimming the tips. If you cut into the quick, the nail will bleed and it will hurt the puppy. Should you cause bleeding, hold a cloth or paper towel firmly against the nail until the bleeding stops.
- Clipping the nails on the back paws can be tricky. You may want to enlist a helper to hold the pup by the collar while you lift his legs.
- Some dogs really, really hate having their nails clipped, and may snarl at you or nip you. These dogs are not good candidates for being clipped at home.

When choosing a groomer for your puppy, the first question to ask is whether puppies are cage-dried or hand-dried. Walk into a lot of grooming shops and you'll see dogs lined up in cages with blow-dryers blasting hot air in their faces. The dogs are freaked out. They can't breathe. They can't turn their bodies around to escape the blast because then they get burned on their little butts. You can kill a dog by cage-drying him.

**6**

# The Brat Zone:
# 5 to 7 Months

**S**eemingly overnight, your sweet little bundle of fur has found a mind of his own. When you call him, he looks adoringly at you—then runs in the opposite direction. When you walk him on-lead, he grabs the leash in his mouth and drags you down the street. He has become defiant and strong-willed. Your puppy has entered what we call "The Brat Zone."

Don't despair if he seems bolder and braver and definitely harder to impress, demanding to be the center of attention—and, just like a naughty child, acting up if he isn't. Don't tear your hair if your puppy, whose brain is now fully developed, has decided that your status as his pack leader doesn't really impress him anymore.

This behavior is all perfectly normal, perfectly predictable—and it won't last forever. Your puppy is trainable. This is just another challenge of puppy parenting.

## Do I Have to Go to School Today?

Not all dogs need formal obedience training, but it does make a better animal. To a large extent, dog training is whatever works for you. There are a zillion books on the subject but—let's face it—your puppy hasn't read one of them.

Now that your puppy is five months old, you must teach him a three-letter word that will keep you from wanting to use four-letter words. That word is SIT. Here's how to do it:

1. Buy some freeze-dried treats at your pet store or grooming shop.
2. Place a treat in the palm of your open hand and hold your hand out so the puppy can smell the treat and get really interested.
3. Place the treat between your fingers and raise your hand above the puppy's head. (Not too high. You don't want to encourage the

puppy to jump.) This is the hand signal. As the puppy positions himself to get his treat, he will automatically be raising his head and lowering his rump.

4. You say, "Sit!" When the puppy's bottom hits the floor, you release the treat into his mouth.

You may have to repeat these steps four or five times before your puppy catches on. Then, but not before, you should give your verbal command, "Sit!" before giving the hand signal. But this time you have no treat in your hand. When the puppy sits, you go and get him a treat as his reward. You'll be surprised how quickly the puppy will learn to sit on command, knowing there's a reward in store.

Teaching this behavior should be fun for both you and your puppy. If the puppy doesn't respond within a reasonable time (four or five attempts both with and without treat in hand), back off for a while. It's likely that both of you are tiring and your puppy will pick up on the aggravation in your voice and will not want to perform. As Scarlett O'Hara said, "Tomorrow is another day." But you must persevere. Teaching a puppy to sit on command is vitally important. It gives you control over your puppy both in the home and in potentially dangerous confrontations with other dogs outside the home.

Using the same technique, you can now teach the puppy more commands—"Stay!" "Down," and "Come." But don't overdo home schooling—two or three sessions a day is plenty. One word of caution: Never use the "Come" command to summon a naughty dog to reprimand him. The dog will remember this forever and will run the other way the minute you say, "Come!"

## Pup's Personal Trainer

You may already have enrolled your puppy in one of the group puppy classes offered through parks and recreation departments and pet stores.

# Kritter Sitters' Top Dog Treats

✔ **Chew chips:** plain or flavored with lamb and rice, beef or chicken. The flavored ones can become chewies from hell, leaving ghastly stains on your furniture or carpet, so it's best to give them to the dog only on a washable surface.

✔ **Bones:** compressed, not rolled, rawhide. High in protein, good for tartar control. Look for those made in the U.S.A., as others may be bleached with formaldehyde.

✔ **Nylabone:** edible bones in a variety of flavors, including carrot, spinach, peanut, bacon, and chicken-cheese. The softer Gum-abone meat- or chicken-flavored plastic bones are easier for older dogs to chew.

✔ **Sterilized all-natural bones:** Fill them with treats such as peanut butter, which all puppies love, and your puppy will be kept busy for hours trying to get out the last morsel.

✔ **Freeze-dried, cubed liver treats:** Great for rewarding your puppy for good behavior during training.

✔ **Dog biscuits:** Don't buy those that are artificially colored. And don't give your puppy more than two a day or you're going to have a very round puppy.

✔ **"Good Boy" Choc Drops:** the only "chocolate" your dog should ever eat. It's a great way for your dog to get his vitamins and protein. Choc Drops look and smell like the real thing—but they don't taste like it. Since they don't taste like the real thing, he'll never develop a taste for chocolate if you give him Choc Drops.

We do recommend these for several reasons. One, they teach your puppy the basics while giving him a chance to meet others his own age. Two, they can help you correct your mistakes and stay motivated.

But now you're thinking about graduate school for the pup. This means a personal trainer. You have two options: group classes and private training. Private training is very expensive, and most dogs do well in a group. Aggressive dogs may do better one-on-one, because in class they are focused only on the teacher, not on those eight other dogs in the circle that they'd love to jump.

Whether you choose private or group training, picking the right trainer is all-important. A dog trainer does not have to be trained—at least not formally—in some university of dog training. You could hang out a shingle tomorrow and anoint yourself a dog trainer. Unfortunately, a lot of people who call themselves dog trainers don't know what they're doing and can instill in your dog bad habits that it will take forever to correct. We do not pass ourselves off as dog trainers or dog behaviorists. But if we chose to, we could put out a sign, take your dog for a couple of hours a day, and take your money. That's one of the downsides of the pet industry. If the trainer you are considering gives you a reference, as he should, check it out. That client may tell you, "Well, judging by the results, my suspicion is that he just sat there the whole time watching television—and then charged me a fortune."

As in finding a vet, word of mouth is the best way to find a good trainer. Veterinarians and pet stores will also make recommendations. Before signing up, you should observe the trainer in action, see how he works with your dog, and how your dog responds. We've seen trainers that dogs just ignore, and trainers that couldn't train a bird. There are others that dogs just go nuts for. Your dog may respond better to one training technique than to another. We think that, above all, a dog should be trained with kindness, not heavy-handedness. You want a dog that is doing things because he wants to please you, not because he's terrified of being hit. There is never, ever, any reason to hit a dog.

# Enough! Don't Overdo It

Whatever you do, don't overtrain your dog. For most dogs, eighteen sessions is probably plenty. You cannot train a dog day in and day out without a break. You have to let him be a dog now and then. Once he has learned his little routines, you should probably put him through his paces once a week, just to jog his memory.

But dogs can be stubborn little devils. One of our clients who was trying to train her Basenji to the lead found that his leather leashes and collars kept disappearing mysteriously from their peg. The poor woman was mystified. Then one day while moving the bedroom furniture around she solved the mystery. There, under her bed, was a king's ransom in leather leads and collars.

We've seen dogs go over the top from overtraining. A male Rottweiler we knew was being trained as a protection dog. Well, the owners, who apparently were determined not to raise a wimpy dog, trained that dog until he went wacko and ended up confined to a pen. He was almost psychotic, not good for anything. What were his owners thinking? You can't have a dog like that around people, you can't have him around other animals, you can't walk him down the street, you can't turn him loose. He's doomed to be in a pen forever. The kindest thing would be to put the poor dog down.

A good trainer:

- Trains with praise and kindness, not punishment.
- Is in control of the dogs, rather than letting the dogs run the school.
- Is not so crazy about a certain breed that other breeds get shortchanged.
- Does not keep dogs in line by kneeing them or by stepping on their paws.

# Sex and the Single Dog

Around six months, a female dog will reach puberty and go into heat for the first time. You'll know because your puppy probably will have a little clear discharge from her genitals and some swelling in that area, and she will lick and lick her private parts. Next, you'll notice a bloody discharge, perhaps just a few drops of blood on your floor, and enlarged nipples. Other dogs—especially boy dogs—will be taking a sudden, intense interest and will want to lick her and, yes, to hump her. And she's in the mood.

By all means now is the time to have her spayed, if you haven't already done so. (Spaying is perfectly okay as early as the fifth month.) Female dogs should be spayed not only because the animal world is overpopulated (a million domestic animals are put to sleep each year), but because nonspayed females are susceptible to ovarian and breast cancer. Besides, it's very uncomfortable for your dog, and very unpleasant and messy for you, when she comes into heat twice a year. Those cute little Bitch Britches aren't always going to prevent stains on your couch and rugs. So, have her spayed and save your sanity. There's nothing worse than a female in heat with about sixty-five male dogs trying to dig under your fence, salivating to get at her. And consider for a moment this statistic from the ASPCA: One female dog and her puppies and their progeny can produce as many as 67,000 dogs in six years! Unless your dog is the last of her breed on the face of the Earth, there is no sense in breeding her.

At about six months, a male puppy discovers S-E-X. His testicles will have descended (this happens anytime from four months on) and his testosterone level will be off the chart and climbing. You'll notice that about this time he will stop urinating like a female puppy, in squatting position, and start urinating standing up. He's going to roam, howl, lift his leg up on everything in sight, and want to mount every female dog he can get his paws on. There is also a health issue. Testicular cancer is the number-one killer of male dogs. We are adamant that, unless you plan to breed your dog or offer him up for stud service, this is the time to have him neutered.

Neutering a dog is not a crime. In our view, not neutering him is. Although some men like to think their dogs are going to be less manly if they're neutered (it's a macho thing), they aren't. A dog isn't going to go, "Oh, good grief, I can't ever hold my head up in the neighborhood again." He's just going to kind of accept it—"Oh, okay, I guess I won't be doing that anymore."

A neutered dog is a nicer dog, a less aggressive and less territorial dog. Don't let your vet muscle you into thinking that a dog should not be neutered until he is a year old. It's perfectly okay to have it done in the fifth month. And don't let anyone persuade you that your dog will not "fill out" properly if he is fixed. Neutering is not going to alter his physique. It's just going to prevent him from pacing frantically around your house in search of a girl dog.

## Hi! My Name's Duke. What's Yours?

Dogs are sociable creatures and, at five to six months of age, your puppy will have had his first series of shots and will be eager to explore with you the world outside his home. He no longer needs to be confined to his own yard for his exercise. Socialization is an important part of his growing up. You don't want a shy dog. He will be happy to go with you as you make your rounds, and it's a good idea to take him on an outing at least three times a week.

Puppies venturing out for the first time are going to be apprehensive. Everything is strange to them. Don't overprotect your puppy. If he retreats between your legs, growling, at some perceived threat, such as his first elevator ride, don't baby him. "Mommy's poor little baby boy, all those big, mean people," that sort of talk is only going to convince him that, yes, he was right to be afraid, and growling is an awfully good way of getting sympathy.

# Dog Park Safety

When your pup is about five months old, it's safe to take him to a dog park. Dog parks are very popular, but they are not safe havens. Far from it. People tend to think, "What could be nicer? All these dogs together, sharing their balls and having fun." That is not reality. This is not Noah's Ark. There are dogs of every stripe, each with its own personality, opinions, and attitude. We've heard too many stories about people taking their dogs to a dog park and being completely baffled as to why their dogs were bitten. Well, it turns out that these dog owners had just jumped right out of their cars and let their dogs loose in the park. Now, there might be fifty strange dogs in that park, and if you have no idea on earth how they are going to react to your dog, how do you expect your dog to know? You don't know, either, whether these dogs might be rabid or have mange or whatever.

Still, some people, including apartment dwellers, have few alternatives to dog parks. If you do take your dog to a dog park, he will be counting on you to protect him. That means keeping him on-lead until he's in a safely enclosed area of the park. And don't let your dog play with aggressive dogs that may suddenly turn on him.

Before taking your dog to the park, make sure he's wearing his ID tags. This is what you'll need to take along: your cell phone in case of an emergency, plastic bags for picking up his poop, and towels and a spray bottle of water for cleaning your puppy up before heading for home. If he doesn't get dirty at the park, he probably isn't having any fun. Water is available at most dog parks, but you should take along a bowl. And taking along your own water isn't a bad idea—especially if you don't want your pup to drink tap water. And don't forget to take your camera to capture your puppy at play.

# G-r-r-roup Dynamics

Socialization is very important at this stage of your puppy's life. Dogs that haven't been socialized can become aggressive because they are trying to protect you, the only person they think they can count on to keep them safe. You've been walking down the street and seen a dog run out at another dog, lunging and biting and snarling and snapping. The dog's doing that because he's confused. Instinctively, he wants to protect his owner, but he also wants to meet that other dog, to investigate him, and he can't because you are restraining him as you instinctively try to protect him. You want to gradually socialize your dog by letting him be around other dogs in neutral situations, such as a local park, where neither he nor his new little dog friends will be defending their own turf. A socialized dog can be taken anywhere without fear of his jumping another dog or taking a bite out of somebody's leg.

You might want to socialize your puppy with a friend's dog instead of taking him to a dog park. If you live in a dog-friendly neighborhood—one that has both sidewalks and other resident dogs—his daily walk can be a socializing experience. When walking your dog, you must be alert to any dog coming toward you. Should that dog appear aggressive, just step off to one side, far enough so that the other dog's lead will keep him away from your dog. If you can pick your dog up, do so. (But remember—no "poor baby, big, mean dog" stuff.) Obviously, if you have a large German Shepherd, you're not apt to try to pick him up. With luck, the owner of the other dog will be strong enough to hold back his dog. When we're walking our dogs, and see a dog we don't know, we cross the street. We've learned that a wagging tail does not always mean a friendly dog.

# I'm No Gym Rat

Puppies between five and eight months of age should not be overexercised, as their bones are still growing. If you've bought a dog to jog with, fine, so long as he's built for jogging. The good joggers include the Labs, the Golden Retrievers, Springer Spaniels, Border Collies, and Australian Shepherds. A deep-chested dog, such as a Bulldog, is not built for jogging, nor is a Welsh Corgi with his little short legs. You can't expect a Yorkie to jog with you—except as a passenger in your backpack.

A puppy under five months of age is probably not quite ready to hit the jogging trail and is likely to just sit down after about fifty feet. Don't rush your puppy. At six to seven months, he will probably be happy to go running with you. But don't run any farther than you're prepared to carry your dog back. We've seen guys out on their bikes, with their dogs jogging away alongside them, until suddenly the dogs just stop cold, like donkeys, refusing to budge. So the owners either have to call someone to come and get them or hail a cab—one with a bike rack, please.

If your yard is escape proof, a puppy five to eight months old will be able to amuse himself there for longer and longer periods of time. Doggie doors, widely available at pet stores and home stores, will give him the freedom to come and go as he pleases. As he is now housetrained, a doggie door will also keep you from having to jump up every time he needs to do his business. You can start teaching your puppy at about five months of age to push the doggie-door flap with his paws or nose. There are doggie doors that slip into sliding glass doors and there are models that can be installed in wood doors. There's even one that picks up vibes from a transmitter on your dog's collar and opens as he approaches. Although it may seem preciously high-tech, it's really not a bad choice if you live in an area where you're apt to have raccoons, skunks, or other critters entering or exiting through your doggie door. For security reasons, get the smallest doggie door that is practical for your dog, taking into consideration that he's not yet fully grown, and install it so it is not visible from the street. We've heard too many stories about thieves enlisting as their accomplices children small enough to crawl through a doggie door.

# Doggie IDs

Sadly, we live in a world where dog theft is commonplace. If you have a purebred dog, you should consider protecting him with some sort of permanent ID now that he is out and about in the world. It goes without saying that you'll want him to wear a collar with ID tags bearing your telephone number. Name is optional. There is always the possibility that a dog thief could call him by name to capture him through trickery. Dog ID tags will likely get a lost dog returned to you. A stolen dog is another matter.

Permanent ID options include tattooing. Your vet will be able to recommend a responsible tattooer. The tattoo should always be on the inside of one thigh, not on an ear, as ear tattoos are much easier to remove. Tattoos need not be expensive. Many communities have animal clinics that on certain days offer low-cost mass tattooing. Your puppy won't particularly enjoy the experience, but it is only minimally painful and—as they say—it's for his own good. There are two downsides: Tattoos will fade in time, and on longhaired or thick-coated dogs, the fur on the area that was shaved when the dog was tattooed will grow back and make the identifying mark hard to find.

Your tattooer will put you onto a national registry that, for a fee, will register your dog's tattoo. If your dog is lost, you notify the registry, which searches its database to locate you. Your birth date or social security number or other set of numbers is a good choice for your dog's identifying tattoo because it is easy to remember.

Another way of protecting your dog, and one that is gaining in popularity, is microchipping. There are several companies making these microchips, which are smaller than a pea and are inserted with a hollow needle just under the skin between the dog's shoulder blades. When you buy the microchip, you get a code that is yours and yours alone. These codes can be read by a special scanner, with which many animal shelters are now equipped. These shelters will routinely scan lost dogs that are brought to them. Just as there are tattoo registries, there are microchip registries. Some, like the National Dog Registry, do both.

Everyday precautions you can take: If your pup is in your yard, be sure the fence is high enough that someone can't just reach over and grab him. Always keep the gates locked. Never leave your pup alone in your car or tethered to a pole outside while you do your shopping.

## Can I Sleep with You?

There are perplexing issues that you will confront with a puppy that is five to eight months old. One of the most perplexing is whether to let the dog continue to sleep in your bedroom.

Just as people line up on both sides of the should-baby-sleep-with-the-parents debate, there are people who always sleep with their dog, once the dog is housebroken, and there are those who recoil at the very idea. We have had clients who wound up sleeping in separate bedrooms because the wife wanted the dog to sleep with her and the husband did not.

We also had a client who was so neurotic about her dogs' safety that she locked all nine of them in the bedroom with her at night. Although we confess that our dogs sleep on our beds, nine dogs sharing your sleeping quarters does seem to us to border on eccentricity. To be honest, just owning nine dogs, unless you're a breeder, seems a little eccentric in itself.

Nothing really bad is going to happen to you or your dog if he sleeps on your bed. You might roll over on him, or he might fall out of bed. The worst scenario is that he might pee in the bed, but that's un-likely if he is walked just before bedtime. Bigger dogs have higher body temperatures and may actually prefer to sleep on the floor, where it's cooler, but little dogs are bed snugglers.

You should know that once you allow your dog to sleep on your bed, your chances of luring him to his own bed—other than by his choice—are zero to none. You've got yourself a permanent roommate. Consider a king-sized bed.

## When Buster Meets Junior

Another matter about which we're frequently asked is how to introduce a new baby into a household with an adolescent puppy. You will prob-ably want to remove the puppy from the home just before the baby is brought home and keep him away for two or three days. Ashley the Bulldog, one of our clients, was well established as the child of her family when—bingo—her owners' first baby arrived. Naturally, they were apprehensive. Would Ashley be psychologically damaged? Or would she try to harm the baby? Ashley was sent to board with us. When we took Ashley home, we introduced dog and baby. No prob-lem. Ashley now sleeps under the baby's crib.

## Pup's Beauty Routine

Now that your puppy is five to eight months old, you want to establish a bath, beauty, and hygiene routine.

✔ Twice a month: Have a high-maintenance puppy groomed by a professional. Examine his teeth for signs of tartar buildup. Check his ears and eyes for discharges that might indicate in-fection.

✔ Once a month: Bathe a low-maintenance puppy or have him
   bathed by a groomer.
✔ Every six to eight weeks: Clip the puppy's nails or have them
   professionally trimmed.

There is one particularly unpleasant little task that you may need to
attend to should you choose to groom your dog at home: expressing
the anal sacs. You're probably wondering what on earth an anal sac is,
though you've got it pretty much pinned down to one area of the
anatomy. The anal sacs are tiny openings at the five and seven o'clock
positions on the pup's butt. They contain a ghastly-smelling fluid that
the dog uses to mark his or her territory. (When other dogs sniff around
there, they're trying to identify the dog.) The sacs should empty regularly when your dog has a bowel movement. If for some reason they
don't, you'll know it because the poor pup will be scooting around on
his rear end, seeking relief. We won't give you a blow-by-blow how-to,
but will tell you that emptying the anal sacs is best done outside. And
don't forget your latex gloves and a large towel to drape over the pup's
rear. Ask your vet or your groomer for details, please.

# I Am What I Eat

We had a client who fed her puppy M&Ms because she herself loved
M&Ms. Well, her dog did, too, but he was lucky to survive such a
"treat."

---

### ☙ DID YOU KNOW? ☙

Onion and garlic contain high levels of a sulfur compound that
in large amounts can damage a dog's red blood cells and cause
hemolytic anemia? Onion rings are not for dogs.

---

## Kritter Sitters' Top Ten Dog Foods

*B*efore dogs were domesticated, they would eat almost anything. They ate what other animals left behind, and they killed to eat. As we well know, dogs are not the most finicky of eaters.

Today, thanks to extensive scientific research, there is a commercial dog food for every dog's needs. The best all-around foods combine grains and meat products. There are dry foods (kibble); canned foods; semimoist foods with a consistency similar to hamburger; premium foods; special diet foods; foods for senior dogs; and foods for dog with allergies, pregnant dogs, high-energy dogs, and dogs that are stressed out.

Here are our Top Ten picks (most are available as a wet or dry food unless otherwise noted):

- **Flint River Ranch,** a wonderful dry kibble. Available by phone (909–682–5048).
- **APD Advanced Pet Diet,** by Breeders Choice.
- **Renew,** by Breeders Choice.
- **Avoderm,** by Breeders Choice.
- **Pinnacle,** by Breeders Choice (Dry only).
- **Innova,** by Natura Pet Products or online at www.naturapet.com. A dry food high in antioxidants, Innova combines poultry, vegetables, fruit, dairy products, and garlic.
- **Eukanuba**
- **Iams**
- **Science Diet**, by Hill's.
- **Nature's Recipe**

Dogs are not designed to eat people food. When we have obese dog clients, we'll confront the owners: "Are you giving that dog table scraps?" Invariably they'll say, "Well, I give him a bite here and there. Maybe a little cheese, or some popcorn, while we're watching TV together." And here's this dog that looks as though he's going to pop. The truth, when it finally comes out, is that the dog is getting eggs and bacon and buttered toast and pork chops. The owner is killing the dog with kindness. If you must give your puppy food from the table, make it an end of toast (no butter, please) or a scrap of a hamburger bun—not your French fries and not the burger. Better yet, don't give in. If you get the pup in the habit of getting table scraps, you're going to have a dog that will sit and beg at every meal and drive you crazy.

# Feel My Ribs

Dogs should not graze. They should be fed on a set schedule, twice a day once the dog reaches six months of age. Don't blindly follow the "recommended serving" advice on the label. Remember, the company makes its money by selling you more dog food. If you cannot easily feel your dog's ribs, he is overweight and his rations should be cut. We feed our adolescent and adult dog clients about two-thirds of their day's quota in the morning. A dog with a full stomach will be more content and far less likely to bark or chew up your furniture while you are at work. Supermarket shelves are stacked high with dozens of brands of dog food—none of which we recommend. Most of it is full of glucose, oils, meat by-products, and so many preservatives that it will be around long after you and your dog are gone. Others have fillers, such as wheat, rice, or talc, to which many dogs are allergic. Food allergies can cause a dog to have diarrhea or to get hot spots on his skin, lose his hair, and scratch, bite, or lick incessantly. If this happens to your puppy, putting him on a vegetarian diet temporarily should clear things up.

Study the labels and steer clear of foods that contain artificial coloring or ingredients with names that would stump a chemistry professor. Here are a few things that you may decide your dog can do without:

- ✔ Meat or poultry by-products. We're talking lungs, brains, intestines, and other things you don't want to know about. These are fillers. They won't hurt your pup, but they provide very little nutrition. When buying pet food, check the ingredients list. If by-products are first on that list, choose another brand.
- ✔ Beef tallow. That's plain old fat hiding under another name.
- ✔ Ethoxyquin. A mysterious-sounding chemical, it is simply a preservative. We are against giving dogs food loaded with these preservatives.

## McKibble

Most commercial dog food is the puppy equivalent of junk food, sort of like having a Big Mac and a hot fudge sundae. Dogs love it because it tastes good, but most of it has zilch nutrients and vitamins. The best dog foods are those you buy from your vet or at your pet shop. When buying one of these all-natural foods (no preservatives), be sure to check the last-sale date. At home, keep the food in a cool, dry place and freeze what you are not going to be using within two or three weeks.

Dogs don't really need meat, although we had as clients two little Beverly Hills dogs that enjoyed a steady diet of venison or duck. And dogs certainly don't need horse meat, which isn't particularly good for them and certainly isn't good for the horse. We feed our vegetarian dog clients Avoderm, an avocado-based kibble that is very healthful. For the others, we buy frozen chicken parts, cook, bone, and shred them, then sprinkle them over their dry food. All dogs love vegetables, such as shredded carrots, which add both bulk and nutrients to their diet. Some of our dog owners add a tablespoon of plain yogurt to their dogs' dry food several times a week to pep it up and make it more moist. Some dogs we know go bananas for bananas.

Whether you choose to give your pup dry food, or a combination of dry and wet food, it's important to be consistent. If you plan to travel with your dog, dry food is much less of a hassle. In any event, if you keep switching between dry and wet food, you're going to wind up with a picky eater. Your puppy may go on a hunger strike, hoping that something better than this old kibble will come his way.

## Does He Need Baby Food?

You may be confused to find that there are dog foods formulated for puppies and for adult dogs. Isn't dog food just dog food? Well, no. The puppy formulas pack in lots of extra vitamins, protein, and calcium. The label will tell you that puppy food is great for the first year of your dog's life, but in truth you should switch to an adult formula long before that, certainly by five months. After that age, the puppy doesn't need the extra nutrients, and too much protein and too much calcium can be hazardous to his health. This is especially true for large breeds that are prone to bone and joint problems.

We have a strong suspicion that dog food companies make all these special formulations just so their packages will take up lots of shelf space. Shoppers do sort of naturally gravitate to the brand that is most conspicuously displayed.

Puppies are not candidates for free feeding. A puppy this age will simply eat until he explodes. We've had client dogs that, if allowed, would work their way through a forty-pound bag of kibble for breakfast and be ravenous again by lunchtime. If for some reason you must leave food out for him—say, you're going to be very late coming home—make sure it's dry food. Otherwise, you will have veritable platoons of ants circling your puppy's bowl.

# Home Cooking

We know parents who eschew commercial baby foods and make their own. And we know dog owners who wouldn't dream of letting ready-made dog food touch their dogs' lips.

In some cases, this is because the dog has a large number of food allergies. More commonly, it is because the owner wants the dog to eat only food that is completely free of preservatives and meat by-products and is low in fat. Most people think it's just too much trouble to make their own dog food and, in truth, most dogs do very well on high-quality store-bought food. Drawbacks to a diet of home cooking: You'll need to give the dog a daily multivitamin. Once he's tasted home cooking, you probably won't be able to get him to eat anything else. Homemade foods tend to be soft and, unless supplemented with carrots or something else with crunch, will not keep your dog's teeth clean.

If you're really interested in raising your dog on home cooking, there are cookbooks out there. We sometimes give our dogs home-cooked food to supplement their regular diet, but we improvise. We might cook up a little ground beef and stir in some cottage cheese or mix steamed rice and veggies with cooked ground lamb, turkey, or chicken.

# Pastries and Pigs' Snouts

All dogs love a doggie cookie now and then, but too many of these treats will throw your dog's balanced diet out of whack and you'll end up with a pear-shaped pup. If you're handing out cookies as a reward for good behavior, two is enough at any one time.

They also love rawhide bones, and those are fine—but not the supermarket variety, most of which are imported and are treated with formaldehyde to give them a shelf life of about two millennia. Pet stores carry sun-bleached, formaldehyde-free rawhide bones that are labeled "Made in the U.S.A." The compressed ones are best because they don't flake as easily and there's less danger of a splinter lodging in your puppy's throat. Rawhides are great for controlling tartar on your puppy's teeth.

You may have seen some items at your pet store that look like pigs' ears, hooves, and snouts. Well, that's just what they are. If the idea alone doesn't put you off, you should know that they are likely to stain your carpet and, if nothing else, will make it smell like a dead pig.

**7**

I'm a Big Dog Now:
8 to 12 Months

**Y**ou did it! You still have your sanity, and under all that fur is a well-adjusted adolescent dog. You took the time, made the sacrifices, and now you're on your way to a wonderful, happy, healthy relationship with your dog.

His daily feeding and walking routine should be well established by now:

- ✔ 7 A.M.:  Walk
- ✔ 8 A.M.:  Breakfast, followed by a walk
- ✔ Noon:   Walk
- ✔ 6 P.M.:  Dinner, followed by a walk
- ✔ 11 P.M.: Walk. Bedtime

From now on, you and your dog are going to have lots of fun together. He's calming down and leaving behind the puppy crazies. His little personality is almost fully developed. Now he is much less dependent on you and can entertain himself and give you a little space— "Oh, all right, I'll pick up my own toy." Of course, he may suddenly lose interest in all those toys on which you spent a small fortune. That's why we rotate our puppies' toys every three or four days. This way, the same ten toys remain "new" and interesting.

But wait, just as you think that at last you have a furry little adult, your puppy will do something ornery. You will command him to "Sit!" and he will look at you as though you were speaking some obscure foreign tongue. Say, "Come!" and he'll hightail it in the opposite direction. Or your housebroken pup may present you with a little gift on your carpet or decide that a table leg is more chewable than his rawhide bone.

He may decide to make a meal of Uncle Herman's pocket watch. Or, if he's a big puppy, he may discover the joy of drinking out of the toilet. People ask us how to stop that nasty little habit, and we tell them

## Are You a
## Doting Puppy Parent?

✔ Do you pull out pictures of your puppy when your friends show you pictures of their children?

✔ Do your sweatshirts or T-shirts have images of your puppy or another of his breed?

✔ Have you ever telephoned your puppy to talk or sing to him?

✔ Have you ever canceled a vacation because you thought your puppy needed you?

✔ Have you ever hosted a birthday party for your puppy and his friends?

✔ Would you give up your puppy if you had to move to better your career?

the only way we know is to keep the lid down. Maybe you could train your puppy not to do it, but we know no one who's willing to sit outside the bathroom saying, "No!" A plumber friend told us the water in the toilet is usually nice and cold, which is very appealing to the puppy. Also, to your dog a toilet is just a nice-sized bowl. (Just remember, if you have a toilet drinker, not to put any of those magic blue cleaners in the bowl.)

# The Trying Teens

What's going on here? It's quite simple. You have a teenager. He's a bit gawky—almost his adult height, but all legs and elbows—and a bit rebellious. On a scale of one to ten, his energy level is a good eleven. Just try to wear him out.

If not kept busy, he may revert to destructive behaviors around the house out of sheer boredom. Until he is about eighteen months of age, he's not to be trusted home alone for long periods of time and should be confined to one dog-proof room or crated. You know what happens when parents turn the house over to their teenage kids, right?

Unlike teenage kids, most of whom wouldn't be caught dead in public with a member of their family, your puppy loves spending time with his parents. And he is old enough to be a real companion. You may want to take him with you to the beach or lake (if local regulations allow), but always on-lead. You may now want to take him camping or hiking. Some breeds, including Golden Retrievers, Labs, Setters, and Spaniels, are good hikers. Little dogs and short-legged dogs, such as Pugs or Bulldogs, don't want to know about it. Don't get carried away when planning your first hiking trip with your dog. You may wind up carrying him back down that hill that the two of you climbed with such enthusiasm. "Enough of this. I'm bored."

## Happy Trails

You should take along your dog's first-aid kit and inside it tape the telephone number of a vet in the area where you will be, or that of a twenty-four-hour emergency pet hospital and the nearest animal poison-control center. If you plan to be in a part of the country where ticks are a problem, you may want to pack a commercial tick repellent. Your vet will be able to advise you, too, about giving your pup a pretrip antitick bath or dip. If you're planning to hike or camp in a state park, check beforehand to make sure your pup will be welcome. Some parks ban dogs.

Taking your dog hiking or camping does not require a major investment in doggie gear. We do recommend doggie saddlebags. Most dogs don't mind schlepping their own gear—portable water bowl, fresh water, doggie snacks, dry food in a plastic baggie, and a wet wash cloth in a Baggie. But don't make the mistake that one of our clients made. A young man who'd never before owned a dog, he was delighted when his Lab, Nelson, was old enough to go camping with him. He remembered to take everything he might need, even a cell phone in case of emergency. We had recommended that he buy a saddlebag for Nelson. What we didn't think to tell him was not to put their food and water, the cell phone, and car keys in Nelson's saddlebag. Everything went swimmingly until Nelson, catching an intriguing scent, just took off, leaving his owner stranded in the middle of nowhere. But the story had a happy ending: Nelson wound up having a fine old time in the company of a kind stranger until Daddy found him.

## Don't Leave Home Without Me

You may want to take your puppy on a long motor trip. By now, he may be well enough behaved that you can let him ride loose in the backseat without worrying whether he will leap into the front and cause a four-car pileup on the freeway. But in our view, it's safer to secure the dog. Accidents do happen. Driving to the park one day, Bosco, a little mixed-breed client, and her owner were rear-ended and trapped in their car when the doors jammed. When the owner was finally able to free them, Bosco fled the scene of the accident, just took off and disappeared. Maybe she was scared, or maybe she just wanted to scout out new territory. Luckily, a passerby scooped up the dog, and Bosco and owner were soon reunited. When Bosco goes motoring these days, she's wearing a safety harness that she can't unhook.

In any event, don't let your dog hang his head out the window, even though that breeze can feel awfully good. A car could sideswipe yours and injure your dog, or something could fly into his eyes and cause an infection. Letting a dog, on- or off-leash, ride in the back of a pickup truck is flirting with disaster. On-leash is probably more dangerous, as the dog could jump over the side and hang himself. If your dog's going to be a pickup passenger, buy him a harness that will keep him securely grounded.

# Dogs and Cars: Potential for Danger

Wherever you go, you should never leave your dog unattended in your car, even for a short time. He may be gone when you return. In every state there are "bunchers," one of the lower forms of human life, who prey on dogs left in cars while their owners make a quick stop, typically at a restaurant, supermarket, or pet store. Bunchers usually travel in large vans with concealed cages in the back. They grab dogs out of cars and sell them to medical labs for purposes you don't want to know about. Another threat is the car thief who may unwittingly steal your dog while stealing your vehicle. We had as clients a cute pair of Cairn Terriers, Harley and Sammi, who loved nothing better than going for car rides. One night on their way home, the owners had to stop for just a minute at a restaurant to say hello to friends. While they were inside, along came these car thieves; Harley and Sammi were off on a wild ride, and it was no joyride. The thieves, having discovered that they had passengers, just dumped the dogs, as car thieves often do. Fortunately, Harley and Sammi were wearing their ID tags and were found by kind strangers, who arranged for their safe return.

Every summer, many dogs die from heatstroke as a result of being left in cars with closed or slightly cracked windows. If the temperature outside is 80 degrees, within half an hour the temperature inside the car can soar to 120 degrees. Don't be fooled into thinking that parking in a shady spot is safe. By the time you return, the sun may have shifted.

Should something unexpected happen, and you must leave your dog in the car—something you should never do except in an emergency—you may return to find him dehydrated. He will be breathing heavily, salivating excessively, or vomiting and hot to the touch. Immerse him in cool water, if possible, give him small sips of cool water, and drive him immediately to the vet.

# On the Road: The Motoring Dog

If you and your dog are traveling by car and will be away overnight or longer, take along his crate—you'll want him in it most of the time on the road—and some of his favorite toys. Pet stores carry a wide variety of portable feeders and water bowls that have nonsplash lids. Some are collapsible. In summertime it's wise to take along a jug of water, a few wet towels, and a thermos or cooler with ice chips.

Some dogs are susceptible to carsickness. As a general precaution, you'll be wise not to feed your dog for about six hours before departure. With luck, you can time matters so that his bathroom breaks coincide with yours.

Unlike in France, where dogs, big and small, are welcome at the snootiest of four-star restaurants, American restaurants permit dogs only at outdoor cafés and, weather permitting, those are a good choice. Otherwise, there's always the drive-through (but no Big Mac for Barney, please). On the road, try to stick more or less to the pup's now-well-established at-home feeding and walking routine.

Today there are thousands of pet-friendly hotels and motels across the United States. Traveling with your dog does not doom you to stay at some 1940s-era motel cabins with questionable hygiene and names like Bide-a-Wee.

Books such as *Pets Welcome* by Kathleen and Robert Fish (see Resources) are good guides, but they don't list every pet-friendly stop. If there's a place that really appeals to you, call beforehand to ask if four-footers are welcome and if there is a charge for your dog.

Once settled in your hotel room, you may want to slip out for a nice long dinner. If so, your dog should be caged. You don't want the people in the next room complaining that his barking kept them awake until midnight. In a place that is foreign to him, a dog feels safer and more comfortable in his "den." If he has been cage-trained, he is not apt to bark. And you certainly don't want to pay for replacing the curtains he chewed up out of anxiety and boredom.

## Up, Up, and Away: Air Travel

While neither Amtrak nor Greyhound allows pets on board, many airlines do. Some will take dogs only as cargo, while others permit caged dogs to travel in the passenger cabins. As airline policies differ greatly, and are constantly changing, you should call the airline on which you plan to travel. You will need a reservation for your dog. Here are the questions you'll want to ask:

✔ Will my dog be allowed to travel in the cabin with me?
✔ What type of pet carriers do you accept? (Even if the clerk at the local pet store assures you that a certain crate is airline-approved, and it carries a tag to that effect, do double-check. Rules change.)
✔ What do you require in the way of health certificates and proof of vaccinations?

Fear of flying can be an issue. Your vet will be able to tell you whether your dog should take a tranquilizer before boarding.

Cargo holds can be cold in winter and hot in summer. The Humane Society of the United States strongly recommends that you not ship your dog by air unless there is no alternative. If you must do so, the society offers additional safety tips:

✔ Use direct flights to avoid a mistake during an airline transfer and to avoid possible delays in getting your dog off the plane.

✔ Always travel on the same flight with your dog. Ask the airline if you can watch while he is being loaded and unloaded.

✔ Do not ship pug-nosed dogs such as Pekingese, Pugs, Bulldogs, and Chow Chows. They have short nasal passages and are vulnerable to oxygen deprivation and heatstroke.

✔ If you're traveling during the summer months, choose flights either in the early morning or late evening, as they will be cooler. In winter, afternoon flights are best.

✔ Attach two pieces of identification to your dog's collar. One should have your permanent address and telephone number, and the other the address and number where you can be reached while away from home. Affix to the outside of his crate a label with your name, address, and telephone number; your final destination; and where you or someone you desig- nate can be reached as soon as the flight arrives.

✔ Give your dog a month or more to become acclimated to his air carrier. This will minimize stress.

✔ Do not feed your dog for four to six hours before departure. Small amounts of water are okay.

✔ Carry a photo of your dog with you to make it easier to find him should he be misplaced.

Every airline has different rules for dogs. Some airlines won't take them at certain times of year; some won't take them at all. Some have size and weight restrictions. Most of those that do take dogs have a limit of two doggie passengers in the cabins on any flight. It pays to call the airline and find out its policy.

If your dog is going to fly with you in the passenger cabin, we think a doggie Sherpa bag is preferable to a hard-sided carrier, although a bit pricey at $50 to $90. Made of quilted nylon, the Sherpa bags have mesh panels on three sides to help prevent doggie claustrophobia, a rein- forced bottom, an adjustable shoulder strap that doubles as a leash, and a roomy zippered pocket for the dog's travel essentials. The bags come in sizes to accommodate dogs up to twenty-two pounds and are approved by most airlines.

## All I Got Was This Lousy T-Shirt

Just as you may not always want to take your kids along on vacation, you won't always want to take your dog, adorable as he is. If he's to be left at home, and you can't enlist a relative or a friendly neighbor to take care of him (or you have imposed on one too many times), you have two alternatives: a professional pet sitter or a boarding kennel.

We may be prejudiced, of course, but we think professional pet sitters are by far the better way to go. There are sitters who will take care of your dog in their home, where he'll have the company of other dogs, and there are sitters who will come to your home. We do both, and we've found that most dogs really love being with other dogs. A pet sitter is not a viable option for a dog that is not housetrained or one that tends to be destructive if left alone, but we're assuming that your eight- to twelve-month-old is an absolute angel.

A pet sitter will come to your house twice a day to feed and walk your dog and will also bring in your mail and water your plants. Obviously, because you're giving this person entry to your home, you will want to get a recommendation either from your vet or from a friend who has employed the sitter.

Just as we interview prospective clients, you, the dog owner, will want to interview prospective pet sitters. You should ask what experience and qualifications the pet sitter has and whether he or she has a backup sitter in case of an emergency. Before signing up, it's vital that you, the pet sitter, and your dog meet face-to-face so that you can observe the interaction.

Your dog may think this new person in his life is the greatest thing that ever happened—or he may take an immediate, if irrational, dislike to him or her, in which case it's best to keep looking. The dog may be on to something.

A boarding kennel may be a no-frills place with basic cages or a veritable doggie resort. In southern California there are cage-free kennels boasting such amenities as pool time, "yappy hour," limousine pickup, and private cottages with TVs and VCRs.

A place near Los Angeles, Paradise Ranch, provides "body buddies," people who will sleep with dogs that are used to sleeping in their owners' beds. Pooches that prefer to sleep alone may do so in rooms furnished with adult- or child-sized beds. That's all very nice, but the most important thing in choosing a kennel is the staff. How well trained are they? Do they really care about dogs, and do they have time to spend with your dog each day? It pays to make a surprise visit to the kennel and look around before checking in your puppy. A well-run kennel looks and smells clean, has dog runs and exercise yards, and plenty of light and fresh air.

## From Flab to Fit

As your dog nears his first birthday, you may notice that he has packed on a few pounds. Remember, dogs of this age need only two meals a day—and no table scraps. An overweight dog, like an overweight person, is more susceptible to heart disease and joint and circulatory problems. We're not advocating that you put your dog on a crash diet, only that you cut back his food intake a little and increase his exercise.

Dogs thrive on competition with other dogs—and it's good exercise. Every community has Flyball, which is the canine counterpart of Little League, right down to the screaming partisan "parents" on the sidelines. Flyball is a team sport in which the dogs jump over four small obstacles, then retrieve a tennis ball and return it to the starting line. There are associations that will tell you where to find competitions in your area (see Resources).

Frisbee is also great fun. Border Collies and German Shepherds are especially adept, but we have yet to see a Frisbee-fetching Poodle or Maltese. Many breeds will play, but it takes a little patience and some training.

## Can Alfie Come Out and Play?

Just as children love being with other children, dogs enjoy the company of other dogs, and at this age, your dog is quite capable of holding his own in canine company. First meetings are always a little dangerous. Your dog will be straining at the leash to sniff the other dog or dogs. You may be a bit tense, but the only real danger is if you encounter an aggressive dog.

Dogs display two types of aggressive behavior—assertive aggression and fear-induced aggression—and either can be a prelude to serious biting. When a dog is asserting himself, his tail and ears shoot up and the hair on the back of his neck may stand on end. He may also be wagging his tail—tail-wagging is not always a friendly gesture—and at the same time growling or barking in a high pitch. If he is fearful, his ears will be flattened and his tail tucked between his legs, and he will be snarling or growling in a low pitch. He may stretch his body to its full length so as to appear larger.

In the dog world, size is not everything when it comes to dominance. We had a Toy Poodle, Mr. Murphy, who could face down dogs ten times his size. His weapon was assertive body language. When your puppy meets another puppy, he may first stare intently and then place his front paws on the other dog's shoulders. If the other dog turns, trying to avoid eye contact, he's telling your dog that he won't accept a challenge. This is fascinating to watch—at a distance. You don't want to get into the middle of things unless the dogs start fighting, which does happen when Alpha dog meets Alpha dog. When two puppies meet, both should be on-leash. At eight to twelve months of age, your puppy could get roughed up by an adult dog. It's best to find playmates his own age.

**8**

# Making Puppy Behave—And What to Do When He Doesn't

**P**uppies are like the proverbial nursery rhyme child. When they are good, they are very, very good, but when they are bad, they can be horrid. Don't despair. Puppies do naughty things. You just have to deal with it and move on. Things will get better as your dog matures. And there are ways to put a stop to behaviors such as jumping up, excessive and inappropriate barking, and destructive chewing.

We do not believe in whacking a puppy with a newspaper or physically punishing him in any way. Hit a dog and the dog will remember it forever. Kick a dog once and he will never forget. Treat him with kindness and he will never forget. So what do you do when your pup does something like ripping up your tax return hours before the filing deadline? You grit your teeth, that's what. And you say, looking squarely into the puppy's eyes, "I'm very disappointed in you." Truthfully, that's mostly to make you feel better. But he will know by the tone of your voice that you're not whispering sweet nothings in his ear. Puppies also watch your facial expressions, just as they watched their mother's face to see if she was smiling or growling.

It's futile to reprimand your puppy after the fact. If he's chewing your shoe and you catch him in the act, fine. Take it out of his mouth, repeating "No!" as you do. But if it's even seconds after he's done the naughty deed, he's just not going to make the connection between chewed shoe and the angry tone of your voice.

When three or four family members are all trying to teach the pup proper behavior, the poor dog can get terribly confused. You say, "Sit!" I say, "Down!" It's a good idea to agree on which commands you'll be using and to post these alongside a list of dog duties for family members.

Puppies are just like children. If Mommy says no, they'll try their luck with Daddy. Stick to your rules, or you'll have a dog with behavior problems.

# Breaking Him of the Bow-Wow-Wows

You can't expect to have a puppy that never barks. Your puppy does not bark just to annoy you—really. Dogs bark for many reasons. Some barks mean "I'm hungry." Some barks mean "I need to go out." Some barks mean "There's someone in my yard who doesn't belong there." It could be the letter carrier or another dog. Or maybe he's answering another dog—"Mommy says I can't come out and play today." In time, you will learn which is which.

Excessive barking—nuisance barking—will not only drive you crazy, but will have your neighbors circulating a petition to get you and your dog out of town. Some dogs, including the hounds and guard dogs, were bred to bark. Others, such as the herding dogs, will bark incessantly if they don't have "work" to do. If there are no sheep to herd in your suburb, a regular game of ball or Frisbee will work off some of that pent-up energy.

Some puppies pick up the barking habit from their littermates and bring it with them to their new home. Some dogs are by nature territorial and will bark excessively to tell dogs that come too close, "Hey, buster, back off." But among other breeds there are problem barkers, just as there are problem diggers, problem biters, and problem chewers. If your puppy is a problem barker, it may be because he is left alone too much and is bored or lonely. Just as a toddler will scream at the top of his lungs to get attention—and will keep doing it so long as he gets picked up—a puppy will bark just to get you to pay attention to him. If the behavior isn't curtailed, he may become a compulsive barker.

# What Makes Sammy Bark?

First, you need to determine what triggers his barking. The most likely causes are isolation and boredom. Dogs are not meant to be kept alone in the backyard day after day while you are at work. Puppies need toys, and they need playmates (you will do nicely). You'll have to do some sleuthing to find out what triggers his barking. Try walking out of the house, closing the door behind you, and finding a spot from which you can spy on him without his seeing you. Does he bark at passing cars? At neighborhood children walking past? At the gardener? If he's reacting to outside stimuli, the easiest solution is to block out whatever it is that bothers him. Maybe you can confine him to a back room, away from traffic. Fighting noise with noise is effective. A radio or television with the volume medium-high will drown out most sounds coming from outside and will also distract the puppy. As we've told you, dogs really like to watch TV.

If you suspect that your puppy is barking during the day, we suggest leaving a tape recorder on while you're gone. When you play back the tape, you'll be able to tell if he's been barking just to be barking, or if there were certain noises that set him off.

If you are gone all day, you might want to investigate doggie day care. A puppy a year old or younger is a bundle of energy and is going to sound off just because he hates being cooped up all day in your kitchen. If your puppy barks nonstop while you are away, there's also a good chance that he's suffering from separation anxiety, which we discussed in Chapter Five. He's barking in hopes that someone will come into the room.

## Manipulative Barking

Some dogs learn very quickly that a well-timed "arf!" or two gets the desired result. Then it becomes a game, one that your puppy is going to find quite enjoyable. Your puppy may start barking the minute you put him in his crate and carry on barking for hours. It becomes a contest of wills. He's betting that you won't be able to stand it any longer and will give in. If you do, you're in trouble. He's now figured out how to get just what he wants—out. You must outlast him. No matter how pathetic he looks, no matter how your nerves may be frayed, don't give in. In time, he will give up and stop barking. After five or ten bark-free minutes, you should reward him. Take him out, play with him, tell him what a good puppy he is. He's going to figure out pretty quickly that barking is not going to get him what he wants.

The puppy that gets plenty of exercise is going to bark less. Get down on all fours and play with him. Walk him around the neighborhood so he can investigate firsthand all those things that make strange noises and can dismiss them as nonthreatening. Wear him out. If you

## Puppy Body Language

Why does your puppy sniff and lick all the time?
When a dog sniffs around, he may be looking for something to eat—or may be looking for information. This is one way in which dogs communicate with one another.

A dog can tell by sniffing another dog in impolite places whether that dog is male or female, whether the dog's been spayed or neutered, where that dog's been. A dog's sense of smell is much keener than ours.

When a puppy goes sniffing around your ankles, he's doing the same thing—trying to get information about you, such as whether you have other dogs—or cats.

Licking can mean many things. Most dogs love to lick and find it very comforting. Some will lick obsessively, much as people with obsessive-compulsive disorder might pull out their hair. A puppy that does this should be checked for allergies. It could also indicate an insecurity problem such as separation anxiety.

Sometimes puppies lick people just to show their love. Or they may lick you because they like the salt on your skin.

do, he'll probably want to take little naps during the day—and dogs can't bark in their sleep.

# Quiet, Please

If you ignore your puppy's barking one time, give in to it the next time, and another time give him a treat just to keep him quiet, he's going to be thoroughly confused and may become a nuisance barker.

"Quiet!" is a word he will understand if you teach it to him. Here's how: Each time your puppy barks excessively, grab him gently by the collar with your left hand. With your right hand, hold his muzzle closed firmly but gently and say, "Quiet!" Repeat this daily for a month. Praise him each time he stops barking on command.

When your puppy tunes up for no apparent reason, try this: Hold out a treat enticingly close to the pup and say firmly, but without screaming, "Quiet!" If the puppy stops barking, he gets the treat. He can't bark and chew at the same time, so you score one point. But the object here is behavior modification. You want to gradually increase the time the puppy must be quiet in order to get the treat. Twenty or thirty seconds is probably a realistic goal at first. In three to five days, just your command, "Quiet!" will be enough. A treat now and then will re-inforce good behavior, but lavishing him with praise—"Good dog!"—will also do the trick. Dogs do love to be praised.

Your puppy may be barking for a reason, but barking excessively. One or two good barks in response to a ringing doorbell, for example, are okay. But nonstop barking for minutes afterward is not. A good tug on the puppy's collar, together with your "Quiet!" command, should get results. Failing that, you can try a little attitude adjustment with a spritz of equal parts vinegar and water from a spray bottle. Have a friend ring the bell repeatedly at thirty-second intervals, spritzing him each time he barks excessively, all the while saying, "No!" or "Quiet!"

Even better is the old penny can, which we told you about earlier for breaking the unroll-the-toilet-paper habit. When the puppy barks and barks, shake the can close to him. Instant silence. Squirt guns are great, too. And if you really want to get your dog's attention, get a boat horn. You may wind up hard of hearing, but your dog will be quiet as a mouse.

The one thing you never want to do is scream at your puppy. He'll think, "Oh, good, we're barking together," and you'll find yourself a partner in a bark-a-thon.

## Collaring Him

There's a great collar with a little plastic gizmo that you fill with citronella fluid. Each time your dog barks, it shoots citronella up his nose. The dog hates it, but it's harmless and we think it's humane. After about twenty squirts, the dog catches on and stops barking. Although studies have shown these collars to be highly effective, there are some savvy dogs that actually can tell when the collar is empty and will wait until then to do their barking.

Then there are bark-breaker collars. They emit a high-frequency sound that is supposed to drive your dog nuts and make him stop barking. We think they're a joke. You know what happens? Most dogs just wind up howling right along with this high-pitched woo-woo-woo.

Finally, there are collars that give your dog an electric shock when he barks. We disapprove of these collars, as we don't think it's necessary to hurt a dog to break his barking habit. And these collars are apt to make a dog anxious and fearful.

Any collars designed to curtail barking should be used only as a last resort. Behavior modification, as described earlier, is the real answer to nuisance barking. A dog that gets a nasty surprise each time he barks may decide he's going to show you and take up chewing or digging instead.

# What Big Teeth You Have

When with their littermates, puppies are constantly chewing and mouthing one another. Once your puppy is with you, he's going to want to do the same thing. You and your visitors are fair game. Fortunately, while puppies have needle-sharp little teeth, they don't have much jaw power and can't inflict a very bad wound. Nonetheless, biting is a behavior that must be corrected. Someday your puppy is going to have plenty of jaw power, and you want to disabuse him now of the notion that biting is okay. When your puppy takes a little nip, do what his littermates used to do: Let out a yelp—"Ouch!" will do nicely—and stop playing with him.

Keep in mind that puppies need to bite and chew and will get very frustrated if they cannot. They may even develop worse biting and chewing behaviors. But you have to set the rules. A hand is not to be bitten or chewed. A chew toy is.

In extreme cases, we've been known to bite back—on the ear. Not a piercing bite, just a nip like the mommy used to give him to keep him in line. This is very effective with puppies that are hand-biters. Just one nibble on his ear and he knows, "Okay, she doesn't want me to do that." Now, we're not recommending that you go around biting dogs on a regular basis. They have rubber rooms for people who do that.

# That's No Bone, That's My Mouse

There are some puppies that, for whatever reason, are compulsive chewers. They will chew anything and everything that doesn't chew back. When you can't be there to watch a pup that has this bad habit, you should give him a toy and confine him to an area of the house where there is nothing for him to chew. If you aren't going to be gone for more than a few hours, the puppy's crate is the best place for him. When you are at home, you can start gradually letting the puppy out of his chew-free zone for short periods of time, no more than fifteen minutes at first, increasing the time only as he shows you he can be trusted.

Even the noncompulsive chewer may at one time or another decide to sink his teeth into your computer mouse or the leg of your couch. Tiebacks on low-hanging draperies are tempting targets, as are your Sinatra CDs. Normally, these dogs chew for two reasons: because they are teething and/or because they want to know what all these intriguing new objects are. Rare is the puppy owner who doesn't have some treasured possession destroyed.

In time, your puppy will learn what is off limits. In the meantime, damage control is up to you. You must teach the puppy what he may, and may not, chew. The first rule of thumb: If you don't want your puppy to chew it, put it where he can't reach it. Second rule of thumb: Don't give the puppy old shoes or socks or clothing to chomp on and then expect him to know the difference between those and your Sunday best. He won't distinguish between them.

The best way to teach him what's off limits is to keep on hand a supply of chew toys. When the puppy latches on to your slipper or whatever—and only if you've caught him in the act—grab the object out of his mouth, stick a chew toy in, and admonish him with a firm "No!" Do the same if the chewable that he has in his little jaws is your hand. It will take a while, but one day the puppy will figure out that he's supposed to chew only those things you give him. If he's hanging on to a forbidden object for dear life, you can either hold him upside down until he drops it (he will eventually) or distract him with a dog cookie or a piece of cheese. Puppies love both and will surrender a stolen treasure in a New York minute for one of these treats. If you're gone all day, don't set him up for failure. Confine him to one small room with his toys and some bones to chew.

Destructive chewing, as opposed to exploratory chewing, is a serious problem. As with biting, barking, and a number of other unpleasant behaviors, it is often a puppy's way of telling you that all is not right with his world. Among the classic causes: teething pain, stomach trouble, boredom, loneliness, pent-up energy. He needs time with you, both playtime and time to learn doggie etiquette. He loves to go walking (and not just on bathroom breaks), loves being brushed and fussed over, and enjoys practicing his commands.

You may be able to control the compulsive chewer by making his favorite off-limits chewables less enticing to him. Try spraying furniture legs with Bitter Apple or painting them with hot pepper sauce. And, as we told you earlier, covering an object of the puppy's affections with foil or bubble wrap may keep him away.

# Toys Are Me

One of the best ways to stop destructive chewing is to offer your puppy a chew toy. You can use chew toys to teach proper behavior. If you catch your puppy with his little jaws around your designer eyeglass case, for example, startle him by clapping your hands and saying, "No!" Then quickly offer him a chew toy, at the same time commanding him, "Drop it!" He will drop the object. Treats taste much better than eyeglass cases. That's your cue to praise him and offer him one of his chew toys and maybe just a little piece of doggie cookie.

We like the idea of giving the puppy his own toy box. Now, this needn't be some elaborate number from FAO Schwarz. Anything that can't be chewed will do. That pretty much eliminates wicker, Styrofoam, or cardboard. One of those big, sturdy plastic storage boxes from a home supply store will do just fine. Leave it open and encourage your puppy to paw through it and pull out favorite toys. At first, you may have to paw through it yourself and dig things out so he'll get the idea. Some people hide a food treat in the puppy's toy box to encourage him to go there. If the toy box is always in the same place, he will in time start going there of his own accord and will find things to chew on that are much more fun than the corner of your Oriental carpet. Until then, you can use the toy box as a teaching tool. If you catch the puppy chewing something he's not supposed to have, take the object away, lead him immediately to his toy box, and help him pick out a toy to chew.

# I Dig It!

Just as puppies love to chew, they love to dig. Your puppy will be spending some time in your yard—though not most of his time, we hope—and he is going to dig.

Why do puppies dig? They dig because they smell something down there, something you can't smell. A gopher, maybe, or a nest of bugs. They may dig because they want to bury a treasured bone. A dog confined to the yard hour after hour will dig out of boredom. Trotting aimlessly around the same old yard day after day isn't much fun. Some dogs will dig a hole to lie in—to keep cool in summer and warm in winter—and may prefer it to that fancy doghouse you just bought.

And, alas, some dogs dig just because it's fun. They love to get in there and get their paws dirty. They love tossing the dirt around and discovering fascinating things, such as worms. In no time, a determined digger can uproot your expensive plants and flowers. Some dogs will focus on one spot and just keep digging a deeper and deeper hole. Others are multihole diggers that will turn your yard into great pyramids of dirt.

What can you do? Well, even the multihole digger usually has a favorite hole. Thwart your puppy by cutting a piece of chicken wire to fit the size of the hole and embedding it firmly in the bottom of the hole so there are no exposed edges. Then place a large rock, some gravel, or a few bricks over the wire. By the time the puppy reaches the wire, he will either be too exhausted to dig farther or he will have lost interest. We've been told that placing a piece of newspaper in the bottom of the hole and sprinkling it with some pungent substance such as cayenne pepper or hot pepper sauce works beautifully. Not only is the smell off-putting to the puppy, but if he gets some of that stuff on his paws and licks it off, he's not apt to forget soon.

If you catch the dog in the act, a good squirt with a garden hose and a firm "No!" is the proper response. The compulsive digger is not going to be discouraged by any of the above ploys, and will likely just go to one of the holes you filled with dirt and start all over again, but most dogs can be broken of the digging habit in one of these ways. Those that can't are candidates for serious sessions with a behavior therapist.

On the if-you-can't-fight-'em-join-'em-theory, we advocate backyard puppy miniparks. Here's what you do: Spread a large square of plastic sheeting on the ground and cover it with some of that grass-by-the-yard from your local nursery. Keep taking the puppy to it and encouraging him to dig to his heart's content. He can't do any harm. You will have to water the sod and replace it when it turns yellow. Some people get fancy and build a sandboxlike enclosure for the puppy park.

# Jumping Jacks

No one enjoys a puppy that greets you at the door by knocking you over and slobbering all over you. You can stop this behavior, and here's how:

Put the puppy on-lead and have a friend open the door from the outside. When the puppy starts to jump up on the person, say, "Off!" and pull the puppy away. Repeat this four or five times and the puppy is going to figure it out—"Oh, no jumping." If you have control, a dog knows it. Lots of praise and a treat will reinforce the puppy's good behavior until it becomes second nature.

If you're around when your puppy makes a forbidden jump, there are several ways to get your point across. One is to go for the squirt gun (yes, you should keep one on hand) and aim for the dog's middle or rear end, not his face. Hitting him in the face is going to make him a head-shy, cowering dog. A few squirts should cure him of jumping on the furniture. Or blow up balloons and place them on the seat of a sofa or chair. When the puppy jumps up, pop one. One pop is usually enough to convince him that this is not friendly furniture. In no time, just seeing the balloons will make him back off. If you can't be at home to do the popping, take masking tape and anchor half a dozen balloons to the couch where the puppy likes to sit. When he pounces good and hard, he's likely to get a nasty surprise. Of course, drop-in visitors may think you're quite the party animal with all those balloons.

## Avoiding Mixed Messages

Behavior modification is not going to be effective if the puppy is getting mixed messages. If he's not allowed to jump up on visitors, or to jump up on the sofa, he mustn't be allowed to do so because you, a visitor, or some member of your family decides it will be okay "just this once."

If all else fails, the wonderful world of electronics has come up with a $30 battery-operated device called Pet Trainer, available through pet supply catalogs. You place the device on your sofa, kitchen counter, or wherever you want to discourage jumping. The slightest vibration sets off a jarring alarm that is supposed to send your puppy fleeing for his life. We can't vouch for its effectiveness, but we see no harm in such a device. On the other hand, we disapprove emphatically of similar devices that rely on shock therapy.

# Getting Tricky

There are those who disapprove of teaching a pup tricks, thinking it's cruel or silly or both. While we think that some of David Letterman's Stupid Pet Tricks are a bit extreme, we see no harm in teaching your pup a few simple tricks. Dogs actually enjoy the attention, and the praise they get for performing. Make it fun for you and your dog. Don't push him too hard to perform or he may balk. "Am I going to be quizzed on this, or what?"

We had a client, a black Cocker Spaniel named Nicky, whose owner, a retired man, had spent hours trying to teach him tricks. Now, Nicky was sweet and lovable, but not the brightest dog on the block. After months of trying, the owner finally was able to get Nicky to sit up on command and balance a doggie biscuit on his nose. Nicky knew he wasn't to touch that biscuit until he heard the command "Charge!" One

## Puppy Talk

Your pup should easily learn these words when you speak them with the appropriate inflection in your voice. He may not speak English, but your body language and facial expressions will help him get the message.

| | | | |
|---|---|---|---|
| • Ball | • Drop | • Off | • Treat |
| • Bath | • Get | • Outside | • Walk |
| • Bed | • Go | • Quiet | • Water |
| • Bone | • Good dog | • Sit | |
| • Bye-bye | • Kiss | • Stay | |
| • Come | • No | • Toy | |

day a friend was visiting and asked if he could have Nicky do his trick. He commanded him to sit, and put the biscuit on the dog's nose but, being a bit forgetful, walked into another room and forgot all about poor Nicky. The owner and his friend went out to dinner and, arriving home hours later, found Nicky, swaying slightly and salivating profusely, still balancing that biscuit and waiting for someone to say, "Charge!"

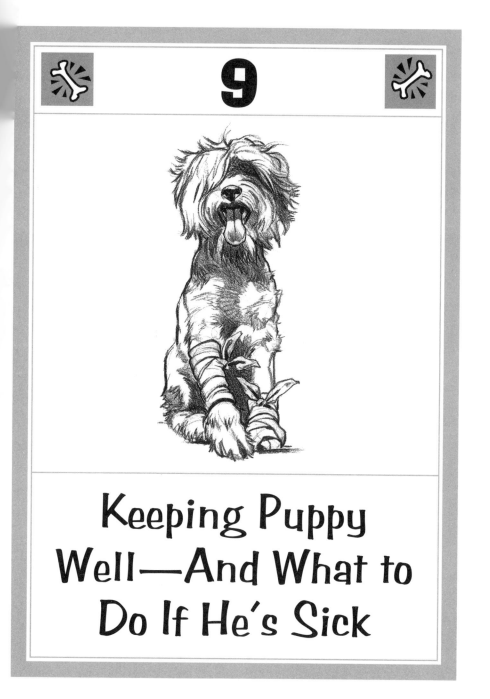

**9**

# Keeping Puppy Well—And What to Do If He's Sick

**P**uppies, like children, get sniffles and sneezes, earaches and toothaches, and a laundry list of ailments ranging from the hiccups (which will go away on their own) to the doggie counterpart of acne.

Just as you watch a child for any sign of illness, you need to watch your puppy. In time, you will be so attuned to him that you will pick up on any little behavior that might indicate trouble. There's a wonderful saying, "Listen to the heartbeat at your feet." Your puppy's reactions, movements, and even the look in his eyes will be different when he's sick or something is hurting.

The first line of defense is, of course, preventive care. That means keeping his shots up to date, having regular checkups with his veterinarian, seeing that his teeth and ears are kept clean, giving him the best-quality food, and seeing that he has regular exercise. Now that you have a puppy, your veterinarian is going to be as important a part of your support system as your family doctor. In Chapter Three we told you how to find a kind, competent vet. When your puppy is sick, you are pretty vulnerable and, unfortunately, there are unscrupulous veterinarians who will insist on aggressive, expensive treatments, even though these measures are not going to extend the dog's life or enhance his quality of life. Veterinary medicine, like all medicine, has become highly specialized. There are vets who specialize in cancer care, heart care, and skin care, for example. If your pup has a serious medical problem, it makes sense to seek out a specialist.

# Puppy's First-Aid Kit

The basic home first-aid kit recommended by the American Animal Hospital Association includes:

- Activated charcoal (available at drugstores), for poison absorption
- Inch-wide adhesive tape
- Antibacterial skin ointment, for minor burns and rashes
- Blunt-tipped scissors
- A child's medicine spoon or, alternatively, a syringe with needle removed (available from your vet) or a plastic eyedropper, for giving the puppy liquid medications
- Three- by three-inch gauze pads and a three-inch roll of gauze
- Hydrogen peroxide (3 percent solution) as an antiseptic and to induce vomiting
- Kaopectate, for control of diarrhea
- Milk of magnesia, for use as a laxative or for poison absorption
- Needle-nose pliers, for removing an object caught in the puppy's throat
- A rectal thermometer and K-Y or petroleum jelly for ease in inserting it
- Rubbing alcohol, for removing ticks
- Sterile cotton
- Syrup of ipecac, to induce vomiting
- Specially curved doggie tweezers, for tick removal
- Emergency phone number for your veterinarian, taped inside the lid of the kit

# When to Call the Doctor

Any of the following symptoms may indicate a serious illness, and you should watch your puppy closely:

- ✔ A fever above 103 degrees, taken with a digital rectal thermometer, available at any drugstore. A dog's normal temperature range is 102 degrees to 102.5 degrees.
- ✔ Loss of appetite for more than twenty-four hours
- ✔ Vomiting or diarrhea that lasts more than twenty-four hours. If the dog is vomiting yellowish bile, or there is blood in either vomit or stool, call your vet immediately. If your puppy vomits once or twice and then seems fine, he probably is. Withholding food for twelve hours should calm his stomach. It's okay to start giving him small amounts of water about two hours after he stops vomiting.
- ✔ Difficulty urinating or having bowel movements and/or presence of blood in the stool or urine
- ✔ Runny nose and/or watery eyes
- ✔ Seizures or convulsions
- ✔ Choking or coughing
- ✔ A persistent limp
- ✔ Difficulty breathing. If you cannot see anything lodged in the puppy's throat when you open his mouth, seek immediate medical attention.
- ✔ Gagging or excessive drooling

Your puppy can't tell you, "Mommy, it hurts," so it's up to you to be alert to any change in his normal behavior that may indicate illness. Perhaps there is nothing specific, but he appears to be sluggish or out of sorts. It is always better to be safe than sorry. A phone call to your vet will put your mind at ease. If there is a serious problem, you don't want to wait until it becomes difficult or impossible to cure.

# The Allergy-Prone Pooch

It's only fairly recently that allergies have been recognized as a cause of puppy maladies ranging from chronic sneezing to ear infections to the canine equivalent of hives. As with humans, allergens that can make puppies miserable include various foods, insect bites, dust and mold, pollens and grasses, feathers, wool, and food additives.

If your puppy is sneezing, wheezing, or coughing, he may be suffering from hay fever. Food allergies can cause vomiting and diarrhea. If you suspect that your puppy may have allergies, he can be tested by his vet, who will pinpoint the allergen. If it's not possible to remove the offending agent from the puppy's environment, he can be vaccinated to desensitize him.

Allergy-related skin problems are common in puppies as they reach one year of age. Symptoms include chewing the paws, scratching excessively, patchy hair loss, recurring ear infections, inflamed red bumps on the skin, abscesses, and blisters. Your vet may prescribe antibiotics or cortisone to relieve the itching. If practical, it's up to you to remove from the home whatever substance is causing the problem.

# Repelling Ringworm

Ringworm is another matter. It's actually a fungal disease, and it is frequently seen in puppies. The head and neck are most commonly affected. There will be flaky red or gray circular patches up to two inches around on the puppy's skin.

Your vet will make the diagnosis by shining an ultraviolet light on the lesions. It's important to catch ringworm early, as it can progress to cover the puppy's entire body and become life threatening. It is also highly contagious both to other animals and to humans. Children are particularly susceptible and must not be allowed to handle a puppy that has ringworm. As a precaution, the puppy's dishes, bedding, and cage should be disinfected with a solution of a quarter-cup of household bleach in a gallon of water.

Your vet will probably trim the hair in the infected area and prescribe a special shampoo and regular application of a topical antifungal cream. Stubborn cases may require a prescription medication given orally for several months.

## Lice and Ticks

You might not want to think about this, but lice may also attack your puppy. Fortunately, lice invasions are uncommon; keeping your dog's quarters meticulously clean is the best defense. What, exactly, are lice? They're little gray, wingless insects that can be seen with the naked eye. There are two types, one of which prefers a diet of your puppy's skin flakes. The other, however, is a blood-sucking pest that causes more damage. Lice do not lie around waiting to pounce on the nearest puppy. Your puppy can get lice only from direct contact with an infected dog.

The puppy that has picked up lice will scratch and scratch, often hard enough to create bald patches. Lice seem to gravitate to the head, neck and shoulders, and anus. Luckily, animal lice—even those little blood-sucking devils—succumb readily to insecticidal dips. And your puppy's lice will not leap onto your kids' heads. As with ringworm, it's a good idea to disinfect your puppy's sleeping area and bedding to prevent a repeat infestation.

Then there are ticks. These look like a black or black-and-red mole until they gorge on your puppy's blood, and then they turn gray. A tick can swell to fifty times its premeal size after a good blood feast.

Ticks can be dangerous. The deer tick can transmit Lyme disease, a threat to both you and your puppy. Deer ticks are most prevalent in the Northeast and Midwest. The disease is potentially fatal to your pup. If he comes up lame and feverish, with no appetite, after romping through wild vegetation or forest, have him checked out by your vet.

Tick repellents—sprays, dips, and powders—are available. Ask your vet about these if you are planning to take your pup into the country. When hiking or jogging, stick to the trails and avoid tall grass where ticks lurk.

Combing your pup with a flea comb will dislodge those ticks that are not already embedded. Ticks are particularly fond of nestling under the pup's legs and around his ears. Those that are already embedded can be removed with special doggie tweezers. Grab the tick as close to the head as possible and pull gently. To protect yourself, wear gloves when doing this. If, once you've tweezed, parts of the tick remain under the pup's skin, that's no reason to panic. Although they can cause inflammation, the parts that remain cannot continue to poison your dog.

Alternatively, you can douse the tick with alcohol, which will cause it to release its jaws. Once the tick is removed, dab some antiseptic or an antibiotic ointment on the spot. Don't crush or burn the tick, as you could release bacteria. Dump the tick into a screw-lid jar filled with alcohol and dispose of the jar, tick and all.

# Ear Alert

The first clue that your puppy has an ear infection is that his ears smell just awful. In addition, the insides of his ears may be red and irritated instead of a nice pinkish-gray, and there may be a discharge. The puppy may shake his head, scratch his ears, or paw at them.

Clean ears are healthy ears. You should check your puppy's ears once a week and swab the inside of the ear folds and as far into the ear canal as you can see—but no farther—with a cotton ball or Q-Tip dipped in hydrogen peroxide or rubbing alcohol or a solution of one part white vinegar to two parts water. Floppy-eared dogs are especially susceptible to ear problems, as it's dark and moist under those long ears.

Bacterial and yeast infections are common causes of ear trouble. Once the diagnosis is made by your vet, who has a special instrument that allows her to peer into the inner depths of the puppy's ears, she will prescribe either an antibiotic or an antifungal medication. Outer-ear infections must be treated promptly, as they spread quickly and easily to the middle ear and can become serious enough to require surgery.

Ear mites are common in puppies. These look like little black specks in the puppy's ears. Mites feast on the ear's inner skin and irritate the ear canal, making it susceptible to infection. The puppy with ear mites will shake his head repeatedly and rub his ears against hard objects. Once infection sets in, there will be a malodorous discharge and crusting of the skin inside the ears.

Mites are highly contagious and can be passed from dog to dog but, like lice, they succumb readily to an insecticide with which your vet will wash out your puppy's ears.

## Doggie Dental Care

Somewhere between seven months and a year of age, your puppy will get his full set of adult teeth—forty-two of them, twenty on top, and twenty-two on the bottom. As these are the only ones he'll ever have, it's up to you to keep them strong and healthy. Yes, dogs do build up plaque, just as you do. It not only gives them bad breath, but can cause gum disease and tooth loss.

You can help prevent plaque by regularly giving your puppy hard dog biscuits, kibble, nylon or rawhide bones, and hard chew toys.

Once his permanent teeth are in place, regular brushings—once or twice a week—should be part of the puppy's grooming routine. Here's what you'll need:

- ✔ A sterile cloth or a special tooth-cleaning sponge or pad or a pet toothbrush, which is ultrasoft and shaped differently from the one you use. You'll find these at pet stores and in pet supply catalogs.
- ✔ A doggie toothpaste. Your toothpaste won't do. Its flavor is too strong, and swallowing it can upset your puppy's stomach. A dog can't rinse and spit. Doggie toothpastes actually come in irresistible flavors like beef, liver, and chicken. In a pinch you can mix up a paste of baking soda and water, which will do the job. But understandably, dogs don't care for the taste and will take much less kindly to having their teeth brushed.

Here's how to brush:

- ✔ Nice and easy does it. To get your puppy used to the idea of having his teeth brushed, you should first introduce the concept of sticking something in his mouth—in this case, your finger. Dip it first in a little beef or chicken broth, then run your finger over the puppy's teeth. After a few days of doing this, wrap a piece of gauze around your finger, dip it in the broth and rub his teeth, using a circular motion. Chances are the puppy will think this is great fun and will look forward to these sessions, especially if he gets lots of praise.
- ✔ Introduce the toothbrush or sponge and toothpaste. You may want to put something the puppy likes, such as peanut butter, on the brush and let him check it out and get used to the texture.
- ✔ When ready to brush, put a little toothpaste on your finger and encourage the puppy to sniff it and lick it. Rinse the brush and put the toothpaste on it.

✔ Lift one side of the puppy's lip and, holding the brush at a forty-five-degree angle, brush the outsides of the upper and lower teeth on that side. Repeat on the other side. Then brush the insides. Be sure to brush close to the gumline, where plaque accumulates. Finally, brush the biting surfaces.

Most puppies don't love having their teeth brushed, but if you start when your puppy's young—right after his permanent teeth come in—he will quickly figure out that this is part of a dog's life. We have a client, a Rhodesian Ridgeback named Ruffin, whose owner started brushing the puppy's teeth when she was only three months old. Now, Ruffin's hooked on the liver-flavored toothpaste and actually follows her owner into the bathroom each morning and waits to have her teeth brushed.

Dogs don't usually get cavities, but some, like some people, are prone to building up plaque. Your vet may recommend one of the plaque-fighting liquids and gels. Professional cleaning and scaling, under general anesthesia, may be prescribed for these plaque-prone pups.

# Puppy "Pinkeye"

By far the most common of puppy eye problems is "Pinkeye," conjunctivitis, an inflammation of the membrane lining the eyelids. It is frequently caused by irritants such as sand or dust (another good reason not to let your dog stick his head out of the car window) or by allergies.

The puppy's eyes will be red and weepy. If a foreign object is the culprit, the discharge is likely to be clear. If the problem is a viral, bacterial, or fungal infection, there will be a thick, puslike discharge that can actually cause the eyelids to stick shut. A puppy with conjunctivitis may squint or paw at his eyes. Frequently, you will see stains at the corners of the eyes and crusting of the eyelids. Because of the threat of infection, and resulting eye damage, the puppy should be seen right away by a vet, who will take a culture to determine the cause and may prescribe either eyedrops or an eye ointment. Some stubborn cases may require treatment with oral antibiotics as well. While the eyes are healing, which may take a week or two, you will want to wipe away the gunk with a wet cloth as often as needed and keep the dog out of direct sun.

Dogs' eyes are different from ours in that in the inner corner of each eye there is a third eyelid with a tear gland. When this gland prolapses and becomes infected, the dog develops a pink protrusion called "Cherry Eye." Most susceptible to this are puppies of the short-nosed breeds, such as Bulldogs, Beagles, Cockers, and Boston Terriers.

Cherry Eye may respond to antibiotics or steroids, given either topically or by injection. But sometimes the vet will have to operate to put the gland back in place. It's a relatively simple operation. Beware of the vet who suggests removing the gland, a once-common procedure that is now frowned upon. When these tear-producing glands are removed, the puppy is prone to developing another potentially serious condition known as "dry eye."

# Bloat: A Potential Killer

Bloat is a life-threatening condition that can afflict large, deep-chested breeds, most commonly Great Danes, Saint Bernards, Weimaraners, the Setters, Standard Poodles, Basset Hounds, Doberman Pinschers, Old English Sheepdogs, and German Shorthaired Pointers.

When a dog is suffering from bloat (medical term: gastric dilatation and volvulus, or GDV), the dog's stomach swells with intestinal gases and suddenly twists or flips over. Without emergency surgery, the dog will die.

Bloat is usually triggered by the dog gulping his food and water and swallowing air at the same time. A susceptible dog should be fed two or three smaller meals daily, rather than one large meal. He should not be exercised vigorously for an hour before and two hours after a meal. Immediately after exercising, he should be given only small amounts of water, not allowed to gulp. After the dog has calmed down, he may have more water.

Because there is some evidence that there is a genetic predisposition to bloat, it is wise to ask before buying a puppy of a high-risk breed if there is a history of bloat in the family.

A dog stricken with bloat has abdominal swelling, retches without being able to bring anything up, and may salivate profusely. This is a medical emergency. Get the dog to the vet ASAP. Severe complications, including peritonitis and heart dysfunction, can develop quickly.

## You Swallowed What?!

Puppies will eat anything that fits in their mouths. If they swallow the object, it will pass into the small intestine, where it can cause big trouble. We've seen puppies eat rubber bands, string, paper clips, sticks and stones, small balls, and nickels and dimes.

If the object makes it down the dog's throat, it can cause an intestinal obstruction. A sharp object may puncture the intestinal wall, and peritonitis can follow quickly. This is another medical emergency. Surgery may be required.

## Open Wide

So your vet has sent you and your puppy home with a prescription medicine and instructions to administer it twice a day—easy for the vet to say. Puppies do tend to resist taking those little white pills and are smart enough to eat right around them after you've cleverly hidden them in their food.

How do you get the pills down? The first hurdle is to get the dog to open his mouth. Here's how:

Place your hand, palm flat, over the ridge of the dog's nose, then close your thumb and forefinger over his muzzle, gently rolling the pup's lips over his canine teeth (those long ones) until his jaw drops. Now, tilt the dog's head down slightly and with your other hand open his jaws. Taking the pill between your thumb and index finger, place it on the center of his tongue, toward the back, then quickly withdraw your hand. The pup will close his mouth. That's your cue to tilt his head up and stroke his throat until he swallows. You'll know the deed is done when the pup starts licking his nose.

Liquid medicines are a little less tricky. Eyedroppers and needleless syringes, available at pet stores, work just fine. For big guys, a plastic (not glass) turkey baster will do. Fill the applicator with the medicine, take the dog's snout in your other hand and tilt his head up. See that nice little funnel-like gap between his canine teeth? Just squirt the stuff in there. This works even with his mouth closed. Again, you may want to stroke his throat to make sure the medicine went down.

## When a Puppy Dies

Losing a puppy can be almost as traumatic as losing a family member. If the dog has been killed in an accident or has succumbed to some rapidly fatal disease, there is shock mixed with grief. But sometimes you, the owner, your family, and your vet together must make a life-or-death decision. This is what you should ask yourself:

✔ What is the puppy's quality of life? Is there too much pain and too little pleasure?

✔ Is there any real hope for his recovery?

✔ Are you emotionally and financially prepared for a long-term medical treatment that may, or may not, help him to lead a meaningful life?

If there are children in the family, a decision to have a dog put down is even more wrenching. The worst thing you can do is to try to protect them from the reality. If they are involved in the discussion, it will be easier for them to accept the loss of the pet. We think that having a child make a donation to a local animal shelter in the pet's name is a terrific idea. The child will take some solace from helping another animal find a loving home.

If you have decided on euthanasia, it is important to keep in mind that your dog will not suffer. The veterinarian will inject him with a tranquilizer, followed by a lethal injection, and he will just go to sleep. You may want to be there to say good-bye. If that's too painful for you, don't feel guilty. Focus instead on the warm, loving home you gave him while he was with you.

There are several options for disposing of the remains. Burying the dog in your backyard is not really a viable one, as most cities have codes prohibiting it. Listed in the yellow pages you will find pet-cremation services that will pick up the dog from your home or from your vet and return his ashes to you. There are also pet cemeteries with pickup service. Or you may choose to have your vet handle the final disposition.

In the days and weeks that follow, you may think you never want another pet, never want to go through that grief again. Or, you may want to bring another dog into your home and your life right away. The decision should be made only after a family council. There is no "right" time to get another dog. The right time is whatever feels right to you. You should not feel guilty, should you decide to get another dog, as you are not replacing the dog you lost. You are getting another one with which to share your home and your love.

# A Final Word

I f you've done your homework, and followed the advice in this book, you have a well-mannered, well-adjusted dog that you can take out among your friends without fear of his being obnoxious. You don't have to spend your life apologizing because your pup is misbehaving. You are a responsible dog owner, one who wants to live with a dog and love him, rather than just possessing him.

Perhaps it's time to reward yourself. Have you thought about getting another puppy?

See Chapter 1.

# Resources

# The Kritter Sitters' Guide to Puppydom

Now that you are a puppy owner, a whole new world has opened up to you. It is a world of books, magazines, catalogs, organizations, and Internet sites, all devoted to dogs and dog lovers.

We would never attempt to compile a complete guide to all that's out there. But we know what we like. We know where to go to find information, or to be entertained, or to exchange ideas with other puppy owners.

Herewith our resource list, starting with—who else?—us. We offer a fee-based pick-a-pup service through which we will suggest two or three suitable breeds for you and help you to find a reputable breeder in your area. You'll find us available to answer your questions at dog-babz@aol.com. Or you can telephone us at (310) 398-8148.

## General Information

**American Kennel Club (AKC)**, 260 Madison Avenue, New York, NY 10016, online at www.akc.org. Devoted to purebred dogs and their owners. Maintains a Breeder Referral Hotline, 900-407-7877, with a listing of reputable breeders throughout the United States. The free *AKC*

*Dog Buyers' Guide* is available by calling 919-233-9767 or writing to the AKC at 5580 Centerview Drive, Raleigh, NC 27606-3390.

**United Kennel Club**, 100 East Kilgore Road, Kalamazoo, MI 49002-5584, online at www.ukdogs.com. The second largest all-breed registry, the UKC registers a number of breeds that are native to foreign countries but, because they are rare in the United States, are not recognized by the AKC, 616-343-9020.

**American Society for the Prevention of Cruelty to Animals (ASPCA)**, 424 East Ninety-second Street, New York, NY 10028, 212-876-7700 or online at www.aspca.org. Has a 24-hour **National Animal Control Poison Center** staffed by veterinarians, 888-426-4435. There is a $45 fee for the first call, and major credit cards are accepted.

**American Animal Hospital Association**, 800-252-2242, or online at www.AAHAnet.org. An association of 12,000 veterinarians, it sets standards for veterinary hospital care and inspects and accredits hospitals. Will put you in touch with an accredited hospital in your area.

**Humane Society of the United States**, 2100 L Street N.W., Washington, DC 20037, and regional offices nationwide, listed with telephone numbers online at www.hsus.org. Offers tips on finding the right breed for you and where to get a dog of that breed in your area, also where to find a good vet. Updates legislation affecting animals.

# Books

Cooper, Paulette, and Paul Noble. *277 Secrets Your Dog Wants You to Know: A Doggie Bag of Unusual and Useful Information.* Berkeley, CA: Ten Speed Press, 1998.
Dodman, Nicholas. *The Dog Who Loved Too Much: Tales, Treatments and the Psychology of Dogs.* New York: Bantam, 1996.
Hodgson, Sarah. *Puppies for Dummies.* Foster City, CA: IDG Books Worldwide, 2000.
Macgruder, Marilyn. *Cosmic Canines: The Complete Astrology Guide for You and Your Dog.* New York: Ballantine Publishing, 1998.

McKinney, Barbara, and John Ross. *Puppy Preschool: Raising Your Puppy Right—Right from the Start.* New York: St. Martin's Press, 1996.

Masson, Jeffrey Moussaieff. *Dogs Never Lie About Love: Reflections on the Emotional World of Dogs.* New York: Crown Publishers, 1997.

Ross, Ruth, and David Weston. *Dog Problems: The Gentle, Modern Cure.* New York: Howell Book House, 1992.

Spadafori, Gina. *Dogs for Dummies.* Foster City, CA: IDG Books Worldwide, 1996.

Tortora, Daniel F. *The Right Dog for You: Choosing a Breed that Matches Your Personality, Family, and Lifestyle.* New York: Simon & Schuster, 1980.

# Magazines

*Dog Fancy,* P.O. Box 53264, Boulder, CO 80322, 800-365-4421

*Dog World,* 500 N. Dearborn, Suite 1100, Chicago, IL 60610, 800-361-8056, or online at www.dogworldmag.com

*Good Dog!* P.O. Box 10069, Austin, TX 78766, 800-968-1738, or online at www.gooddogmagazine.com

Dog magazines report on products such as food, toys, and treats, and give product ratings and warnings. They also provide a forum for readers to discuss dog-raising tips and training and behavior problems.

# For the Traveling Dog

*Pets Welcome*, by Kathleen and Robert Fish, Bon Vivant Press, 1998, is a great guide to dog-friendly hotels and motels nationwide.

# Finding a Good Boarding Kennel

**American Boarding Kennels Association**, 719-591-1113, or online at www.abka.com. Founded by kennel operators, the association offers voluntary accreditation indicating a member facility meets association standards for safety and quality of care.

# Finding a Good Pet Sitter

The following accredited pet sitters have completed required courses and have agreed to abide by certain codes of ethics:

**National Association of Professional Pet Sitters**, 336-983-9222, or online at www.petsitters.com

**Pet Sitters International**, 800-268-SITS, or online at www.petsit.com

# Dog Rescue Agencies

**American Society for the Prevention of Cruelty to Animals (ASPCA)** keeps track of adoptable dogs nationwide, including purebreds, and posts them, some with photos, on its website, www.aspca.org.

**AKC National Breed Club Rescue Network**, online at www.akc.org/rescue.htm

# Dog Fun and Games

**North American Flyball Association**, 1400 W. Devon Ave., #512, Chicago, IL 60660, or online at www.flyballdogs.com

**Alpo Canine Frisbee Information Line**, online at www.discdog.com

# Pet Loss Support

The **ASPCA** maintains a free 24-hour bereavement counseling hotline. To access, call 212-876-7700, x4355.

# Surfing the Dog Web

Type in "dog" on your computer keyboard, and the World Wide Web will lead you to dozens of sites—sites selling dog products; chat rooms; sites offering advice on dog health, behavior, and training; as well as just-for-fun sites for you and your dog. As these seem to appear, and disappear, with astonishing speed, we are reluctant to list specific ones.

# Dog ID Registries

**National Dog Registry**, (800) 637-3647, or online at www.natldogregistry. com. Registry service for dogs that are tattooed or have identifying microchips.

# Pet Supply Catalogs

There are pet supply catalogs galore, most of which offer more or less the same merchandise—some higher-end than others—and usually below pet store prices. The following are some we have used and can recommend:

**Cherrybrook**—800-524-0820

**Allpets**—800-346-0749

**The Dog's Outfitter**—800-367-3647

**Doctors Foster & Smith**—800-826-7206, or online at www.drsfostersmith. com. This company, operated by veterinarians Foster and Smith, offers a full range of products, including some they developed.

**JB Wholesale**—800-526-0388

**KV Vet Supply**—800-423-8211

**Pet Warehouse**—800-443-1160

# Index

rewards in, 20, 64–65, 88–89, 93, 109,
  119–20, 121
role of physical build in, 20, 21, 22
role of temperament in, 20, 21, 22
starting time for, 105
trial and error in, 20, 91
  *see also specific commands*
trash cans, 58
treats, 20, 64–65, 88–89, 93, 109, 119–20,
  121
tricks, 167–68

United Kennel Club, 43
urinary tract disorders, 35, 36, 90
urination, 124
  accidents with, 6, 43, 68, 70, 72, 87,
    96
  difficulty with, 173
  frequency of, 82, 87, 89–90
  odor and, 70, 95, 96
  *see also* elimination; housebreaking

vacations, 4–5
  with puppies, 143–49
vacuum cleaners, 61
vegetables, raw, 65, 135–36
veterinarians, 47, 111, 183
  advice from, 64, 67, 122, 132
  cost of, 10, 36, 42, 74
  referrals by, 45
  regular checkups with, 10, 13, 49,
    50–51, 69, 73–74
  shots by, 10, 13, 46, 47, 50, 73, 105–6,
    111, 147
  treatment by, 58, 73, 171–82
vigilance, 27
vision, 103
  loss of, 26, 36
Vizsla, 12, 31
vocal tone, 77, 104, 167

voice boxes, removal of, 22–23
vomiting, 146, 173

walking, 10, 12, 13, 68, 84, 98, 141
  on-leash, 82, 91, 93, 95–96, 119, 126,
    127
watchdogs, *see* guard dogs
water, 66, 67, 74, 92, 97, 146
water rescues, 28
Water Spaniel, 20
Weimaraner, 12, 14, 20, 31
Welsh Corgi (Cardigan), 30
Welsh Corgi (Pembroke), 30
Welsh Springer Spaniel, 31
Welsh Terrier, 12, 33
West Highland Terrier, 12, 21, 26, 32, 36
West Highland White Terrier, 33
Wheaten Terrier, 12, 23, 104
whining, 30, 83
Whippet, 32, 104
wicker baskets, 62–64
Wirehaired Pointing Griffon, 31
Wirehaired Terrier, 80
work, at home, 16, 56
work ethic, 28
Working Dogs, 17, 27, 28–29
worming, 46, 73, 106

X-rays, 43, 46

yards:
  chaining puppies in, 13–14
  dangers in, 58
  digging in, 32, 56, 164–65
  escaping from, 56, 59
  exercise in, 18, 24, 128
  fences and gates in, 58, 59, 130
Yorkshire Terrier, 11, 12, 34, 128

Zodiac, 112

# About the Authors

**Jan Greye** and **Gail Smith** have been taking care of people's pets for more than fifteen years and specialize in dog care. They are the proprietors of The Kritter Sitters, and are less formally known as the Beverly Hills Dog Divas because so many of their clients live in the 90210 zip code. They offer a fee-based pick-a-pup service through which they will suggest two or three suitable breeds for you and help you find a reputable breeder. E-mail them at dogbabz@aol.com, or call 310-398-8148.